CASTLE GROTESQUE

By: Mike Collins

CHAPTER 1.

  I fumbled through some parchment that lay on my desk and found my pipe at last. Head throbbing and hands shaking, I lit the content and exhaled a puff of smoke into the candlelight. Shapes formed into a cloud, and I could picture the spirited ghosts of my slain cattle lingering in the wind. Each morning was like the last, silent, and corrupt - like a drunken fool's night of debauchery, my head rang in a sea of vile thought. long has it been since regret fell upon my spirit and it would not fall on this day either. A maelstrom of atrocities had its go at me but to no avail; I wiped the burning sensation searing in my eyes and coughed a small fit, not yet amused with my awakening. I reached for the crystal bottle and poured the biting red liquid into my goblet. I desired relief from the misery pounding at my temples, a soothing remedy for the insufferable pain – I took another draw from my pipe and stared at the small gathering of water built up at the corner of the stone wall, but I did not take in the observation. Distraction was not welcome in my current state; I rotated my fingers, grinding them into my temples and pressed upon my eyes with force and slunk deeper into my chair. As I lifted my cup, I ignored the vomiting urge as I emptied the content into my rotting gut, falling my head upon the table and shutting my still troubled eyes. I smashed my fist into the table and rose to my feet.

"Is this your will of me oh Lord?" I cursed! Enraged, I tore off my robe and proceeded to the washroom.

The water burned at my flesh as I submerged entirely into the steaming liquid.

"AAAAHHHHH" I agonized. "Is this your will oh Lord?"

My skin pealed, but before it could tear open, I pulled myself from the cauldron and crawled the stone floor; blisters started to burst, and a small trail of blood followed me as I grazed around my castle floor like cattle.

"For you Father!" I shouted in misery.

Pitiful spirit I have, like a wretched pig wounded and demon possessed I crawled.

"Send me stampeding over the cliff Father, I beg you" I cried.

My cries echoed down the hall as I made my way back to the bottle.

I cackled in desperate release, a fools laugh, delighting in the intense pain self-infliction can only bring. I pulled the bottle from the table and chugged at the red wine inside.

"Ha Ha.. Ha..Ha Bless you Father" I smiled as I fought for air.

I shut my eyes and wallowed in the intensity. The alcohol slowly masking the intolerable pain; I pressed my head into the cold stone and waited for the booze to take fuller effect.

"Take me Father, show me your kingdom oh Lord" I whimpered.

I let out a sigh of relief as intoxication gently floated in.

"Ha ha ha, ha … haha… Blessed be" I announced with peace.

I rose to my feet and pulled up my black robe from the floor and tugged my way back inside. I sat once more at the table and flirted with my newly gained atmosphere.

As my air intake began to steady, I decided it was best to begin morning worship. I pulled another container of alcohol from the table and made my way over to the worship room.

I fell to my knees and took a deep swing from the bottle and began my confession.

"Father, have I not been a good servant to you? How much more can one monk humble himself to you, my God? I have devoted my life to solitary confinement, and this is my will to be? I carry out your will do I not Father?.... CONFESSION!... I am a mere man am I not, HOW?... HOW can I please thee? The torment of the day is not enough that you wish me to inflict more trauma?... This is not about the Cattle, do not reduce me to them! What does thou see in me?"

Again, my desperate pleas were met with silence.

"AAAHHHHHH!! Hear me now oh lord for my tolerance is at the threshold of emptiness, I beg you with a final cry... WHAT DO YOU WILL OF ME?"

I was met yet again with the sound of silence.

"As I thought... As I thought." I mocked.

I stumbled from the worship room and began rummaging through drawers looking for my tobacco. When I neared the kitchen, I was successful in my search just before entering to make breakfast.

After a long draw at the pipe, I pulled a big slab of fresh meat from the smoker and began cutting myself off several slices and made my way to the table and sat and ate.

I did not receive the news in my location - I resided deep in the forest known as Ehpoe Forest; most dared not travel. The surrounding peasants believed these woods to be the gateway to hell itself; I however referred to the place as home.

So, I sat chewing and savoring each bite as I viewed the morning as a special time of relaxation and contemplation before the rigors of the day would weigh in.

"Father Guide my feet" I prayed as I chewed, "Let thy will shine through me oh Lord... For your will is my only desire, in the name of the Father, Son and Holy Ghost amen."

As I finished my plate of meat, I wiped any mess that may have formed in my beard and excused myself from the table.

It was that time of the day when I went and spent time with the cattle. The Lord commands that we should not be Lazy but to work and bring his will to others who need him desperately. I was a vessel from which the Lord was able to do his bidding and I never let my God down.

CHAPTER 2.

My footsteps tapped down the stone steps until the creaking of the door opened into a large chamber. shackles rattled and sorrowful moans floated like a musical passage into my ears upon entry into the dungeon. I grabbed the wooden bucket hanging off the hook above a large tote of food scraps and shoveled the slop into my bucket and made my rounds feeding the cattle.

I had a variety of shapes and sizes. One cell filled with the fatty cattle, another with beautiful women; I had children of all type, men of all type, women of all type you dream it, I got it. a collection obtained over the years – I now an old man, you can imagine the potential. Weather lost or seeking, all cattle arrived upon their own free will, I attribute their arrival as a gift from the Lord.

I watched like clockwork as the cattle rushed the trough and fought and kicked for their share of the food. I had no emotion towards the subhuman, I paid no mind to their desperation.

Twenty-five cells and finally I hung the food bucket back on its hook. I pulled a lever near the only door to the chamber and the water in each cell drained to the outside world. I pumped the leaver next to the drain lever and fresh water filled their barrel that was provided in each cell. Each barrel held ten gallons of water and was replenished every day. Although they were mere cattle, I always made sure they were fed and watered properly for the longest life possible.

I shut the door and was met with abrupt silence. The tapping of the stone reverberated off the walls as I climbed back up the stairs and into the main hall.

As I walked, I was startled by the clanging of a rusty door knocker smashing into steel repeatedly.

"Lord" I whispered softly.

The door creaked as I opened to see a young woman before me. Golden hair and stunning blue eyes, her body that of a Goddess and at quick glance appeared to be alone.

"You" She began. Her dress appearing to be of higher class, it twirled as she spoke. A look of excited disbelief upon her face, I stared without perceivable care.

"You're him" She continued. Again, I remained unreadable. "Please, may I come in?"

I stepped aside allowing the door to open a touch more and ushered her inside.

We made our way to the fireside room, and I offered her a glass of wine and a comfortable chair.

"I can't believe the legends are true then" She rambled excitingly "You can't imagine the time I had finding this place; I was starting to believe it impossible."

I stared without expression as she continued.

"I ran away you know; my father was willing to pawn me off to the wretched king's son – a horrible, ugly man! I had heard stories of this place; most believed them to be mere hoax to frighten the misbehaved but…"

She paused and locked her eyes into my own. Although brief in its romance, eternity was felt in those seconds.

"Do you speak?"

I debated the notion with intense thought; I never allowed the subhuman the honor of hearing my voice. But this women was different, and the Lord assured me It was not lawlessness to respond.

"Child, what is your intentions here" I continued to lock eyes and show no other expression.

"Well... I just"

"If the stories you speak of were to bring fright, as to keep one away, why have you then come to my home?"

She held her eyes on mine, and I could see the battle for confidence well up inside her, until she finally managed to find strength.

"The potential of death is better than insufferable slavery." She said firmly.

"Really?" I finally cracked and let out a smile wrinkle in the corner of my lips. I reached for the bottle of wine and poured us another cup.

"Tell me child, what do you know of death that you should believe slavery is to be looked upon as inferior?"

"The dead know nothing, sometimes nothing Is better than the emptiness of life."

"Interesting" I again gave a grin.

I began to feel my sexual desires flood in and although I tried to keep my emotions at bay, as time unfolded it became increasingly more difficult to resist my urge.

"What are your plans my dear?"

"Well, I traveled so far in the most horrific country, I was hoping to stay a while... or perhaps permanently?"

I gave no expression to the concept and instead allowed my mind time to contemplate the potentials.

"Are you alone or do you have a family?" she relaxed her demeanor and attempted a more casual approach.

"Alone" I answered without hesitation.

"I see, I also am alone" she lost eye contact.

"child, I do not take kindly to psychological games, is that clear?"

"Of course, I just was trying to make conversation that's all." She began to bounce her right leg in a nervous kind of twitch.

"Hungry child?"

"Starved!" she stopped her nerves and locked eyes again.

"Follow me."

We made our way into the kitchen, and I sliced off a large helping of meat and sliced up an apple and presented the meal to her on my best plate.

"Thank you, thank you" She praised as she began to devour.

I watched her eat and poured her another round of wine and didn't say a word. I was taken away by her beauty and the desire to be her own without any consideration of conformity – it being completely out of the question.

"This food is delicious, I haven't eaten in two days, I ran out of food from what I had brought with me on my journey here, I thought I may never eat again."

I believed the wine was beginning to take effect as she started to talk more without purpose.

"You know it took me a month to find this place, I stole a horse and after the third week it was attacked by wolves and I had to walk the last week, there's no need to worry though I wasn't followed I'm sure of it. I had a chamber made locked in my room and I set fire to the place, I'm certain they believe me dead." She ate as she rambled.

"How was that for you?"

"Mmm, I didn't give it much thought honestly, it was just what I had to do to get away… you know you should talk more you make me feel like I'm annoying, I don't like it" she smacked her lips and tore into another chunk of meat.

"I haven't conversed much in the past twenty years or so, I'm not accustomed to it."

"How did you end up here?" she asked.

"Another time." I made clear.

She finished her food, and I escorted her down the hall and into a guest room.

"You may sleep here; you are not to wander is that clear?"

"Yes, may I look about the room?"

I did not respond as I knew she would do so regardless of my answer.

I slipped backwards out of the door and locked it behind me to assure she would not go where she was not permitted.

I swiftly made my way into the worship room and crashed to my knees and lifted my folded hands above my head and buried my face into the stone floor.

"Lord why does thou tempt me, is this your work Father or the work of the devil?" I pleaded as I wept. "surly thou would not bring thy servant a tempest without reason?... I beg you oh Lord, show me your intentions."

I was met with silence and removed myself from the worship room so as not to taint the atmosphere with my lack of understanding.

Enraged once again, I climbed the stairs to the tallest tower of the castle and pushed through the wooden door and looked out the window into the dark forest from whence the child came.

The stars sparkled above, and the moon was captivating illuminating the night sky; wolves howled, and the trees blew gently in the north wind. So vast the wilderness I could see nothing more.

I stood staring into the forest and my mind was rabid with thought. what to do? Is this a test from the Lord? If so, what is the proper course of action? I felt the sexual desire engulf my senses and I disrobed and began to beat the demons lust away to no satisfaction.

I ran down the long stairs, shoved open the door into the dungeon, and walked down to cell number fifteen.

I grabbed a young brunette by the throat and pulled her from her cell and forced her into a small section of the room near the door behind a small wall that separated the view of the cells. I smashed her skull into the stone floor and pulled up her ragged garment and penetrated her tight ass. I squeezed her throat tighter so she would not let out a scream and just before she lost consciousness, I released my grip and her gasp for air made me release my seed inside her bowels. She began to let out a sob but before she could let loose, I smashed her head repeatedly into the stone floor until life left her now limp body.

In the grips of ecstasy, I collapsed to the floor as well and stared into her dead eyes.

"Blessed be the name of the Lord God" I whispered.

I gathered myself up off the cold stone and began slicing sections of meat from her corpse and carried them off to the kitchen to marinate for breakfast tomorrow morning. The remaining portions left on her bones I simply tossed in with the fat cattle to enjoy.

I poured myself another cup of wine and thanked the Lord for another blessed day.

CHAPTER 3.

An intolerable banging woke me from my dreams. I was quickly reminded I had locked the door to the guest room and my new visitor was demanding release. Her hollering voice shrill and piercing.

I slugged down the hall and felt the throbbing vein in my head grow rapid as her voice became louder. As the key turned and the lock freed, the door tore open, and she began her vocal symphony once more.

"Trust issues I see, I merely went to sleep I was overwhelmedly exhausted!" She went on. "Why do you look as though you got beat up in a butcher house?"

I looked down and realized my robes were caked in dry blood and chunks. I did not let this change my vacant attitude in the slightest.

"Meat was low, I spent the late hours gathering us breakfast."

"Oh," She respond, "How kind of you, my apologies… shall we then?"

I followed her down the hall to the kitchen, her joyous prancing was not pleasing to say the least.

As we began to eat, she rambled per the norm.

"This meat isn't as good as yesterday's meat?" she complained.

"Less fat" I commented.

"I see… my name is Victoria by the way, in case you were wondering?"

"I wasn't"

"… do you have a name?"

I continued to eat, paying her no mind.

"The people in the kingdom call you Beelzebub, is that really your name?"

"No"

"May I please know your name?" She asked with a stern disposition.

"I never received a name, I am a monk for the Lord God, his Servant… I have no name."

"Oh, May I give you a name?"

I did not engage in her silly game but continued with my breakfast.

"May I call you Edgar?"

"No"

"William?"

"No"

Before I could listen to another absurdity, I knew I had to intervein, or the torture would never end.

"You may call me Monk, no more… please, eat."

She shuffled in her chair and glared at her plate.

"Just one more question then?" she pushed. "How old are you?"

"Roughly forty years old"

"I'm nineteen you know; you look much older sorry to say… the long hair and scruffy beard does not help…"

"Enough talking!"

"How will we get acquainted otherwise?"

I locked eyes with her, and my mind flurried in anxious desire to end conversations.

"Allow me then a question" I purposed with serious glare. "what if any is your use besides words?"

"What do you wish of me?"

I had a desire, but I was hesitant to bring forth my wishes. What would God will of me? I feared to step out of line. I asked the Lord in small minded prayer for an answer. It wasn't long before permission was granted.

"I believe my time is nearing, I need someone to carry on my work. Tend to Gods will and duties performed in this castle... perhaps."

"You need an heir; I would be honored." She interrupted.

"A female does not carry out the work of the almighty." I stared intensely into her eyes.

"well then, I don't understand…. OH… Hmm… Well I." she stuttered as her eyes fell to her plate. "I mean I just fled a kingdom for the same sake. I wish to be more than a child barer."

"You would bear a child who would carry out the will of God. Do not compare this opportunity to that of a mere peasant birth.

She collected her wits and attempted to change the subject.

"Might I ask my role, beyond motherhood?"

"Fair question I suppose… you ran away from a prince; at a point you would be queen; ruler of a kingdom yet your dissatisfaction brought you here… what then do you deem a glorious life?"

"Freedom."

"What is freedom my child?"

She was hesitant to answer – I believed she had no answer.

"Lawlessness from God is your desire?"

She locked eyes with me again and I could see a whores tongue begin its foul work of deception; But… I was surprised yet again.

"There is no freedom in lawlessness, I only wish to break free from the monotony of man's conformity."

"So then?" I gave a slight grin.

"… Very well, if it be Gods will, I mean I am here, must be a miracle… but I ask that you open up more and share your feelings, I will not be with a man who hides like a coward."

"I will do what I can."

"Fair enough, as you'd say… I refuse to call you monk; can we please decide on a name."

"I will ask the Lord to reveal to me a name when he reveals it you will be made aware… now please finish your breakfast."

I poured a cup of wine and begged for the pounding headache to subside. I knew I needed the right frame of mind for the afternoon activities.

We cleaned our plates and made our way down the long hall, and both entered the guest room. The walk felt long, and my mind swirled in discomfort; she began to pull her dress above her head and my breath vacated from my lungs as I beheld the most perfect body I had ever seen. She crawled just at the edge of the bed and motioned me over. I was hesitant, I took small steps and prayed to the lord for confidence. She rose up to help me disrobe and I clenched her wrists and signaled them back to the bed. She faced forward as I exposed the burnt flesh of my body – never fully disrobing. I slid deep inside of her and felt her ass bounce off my hips. She moaned in ecstasy and my breathing grew heavy; the time elapsed until I finally emptied inside her. She fell to the bed, and I hurried out of the room and hastened my way to the worship room.

"Blessed God in heaven the act is complete, the child now finding the womb will be your servant oh Lord. Father, am I so bold as to ask a name? for the child and myself dear God? Forgive my proud spirit. I am overjoyed in the carrying out of your will Father."

I felt what I believed to be the Holy Spirit enter the worship chamber. as quickly as the spirit filled the room, so too did it abandon.

"I shall remain nameless; the child shall be called Mark. Thou will be done!"

I crawled backwards out of the worship chamber as per Gods command.

Victoria was waiting and she looked enthused.

"Well, what did the Lord say?"

I was not yet able to speak; instead, I took her hand, and we walked to the front door of the castle and made our way outside.

We sat on the steps in the direction leading to the dark forest and I made it clear we did not look towards the castle during out discussion.

"The Father has bestowed upon the child the name of Mark and wishes me to remain nameless."

"Mark?... I suppose that is fine with me..." she began to ramble.

"Enough, we never question the will of God. Mark will be the name of the child and no more thought shall be given." I said with sad sternment.

"Alright, alright... Do you feel the Lord will ever give you a name? and what harm could it do if I was to just call you by one?"

I ignored her blasphemy and stared into the night sky, dwelling on my duties as a husband and father to be.

"Nine months is a long time of waiting, I can't wait to get to know you more… sex was nice, wasn't it?" she tried getting a reaction out of me to no avail. "Kind of hurt for a moment but then got better later on… perhaps next time it will just be fun the whole time? Iv'e never done It before so I can't say for sure."

I continued my stare into the stars and watched my breath vapor into the cold air.

"The day went by fast, didn't it? Felt as though we were just having breakfast and now the stars shine in the sky; beautiful night." She reached out and took my hand – again I remained bound in my own world.

"It's funny, my mother and father dreamed of this moment – of course me with prince Ambrose; such a stupid name. I almost wish I could see the disappointed look on their faces…"

"Marrlage is simple in the eyes of the Lord; we are already as one." I finally muttered.

"Oh, Good… Is there a last name I can now go by?

“No, Victoria is your only title and Mark shall be the name of the child only.”

“My last name at birth is Hannabelle but, I always felt it meant nothing to me… I now see why.”

She fixed her eyes on the full radiant moon, and we finally had a time together in silence. I was no longer tense and finally we allowed the cold night air to embrace our being. I hadn’t felt any degree of peace in all my life aside from this very moment.

CHAPTER 4.

Victoria slept and I made my way into the dungeon. I shut the door quickly, locking it behind me as the cattle barked in chaotic mass.

"Now listen all, the Lord has spoken unto me!" I commanded. "I am to cleanse the sanctuary – to baptize with fire an offering to the Lord."

Fear echoed throughout the chamber.

"SILENCE!" I marched slowly down the hall and peered into each cell. "Count it as a blessing... thou should be grateful" my eyes cut through their spirit, and I watched their tears fall to the cold stone floor. I felt no sympathy - for the subhuman must be shown no pity, they are a resource for God, and I have been given dominion over them as is his will.

"You" I pointed at a strapping man in cell nine; roughly thirty years old and I believed him to be the leader of a possible party who wished to escape my castle - I could see him plotting with the others with presence of authority. "Thank you for volunteering."

"YOU BASTARD!! I WILL NEVER SURRENDER SO EASILY!" He spat.

I walked over to a table near the door and picked up a wooden club from the table and walked back to cell nine.

"Place your head between the bars" I ordered.

He hurled another glob of spit into my face, and I gave him no expression.

"The rest of you back, or you'll all die... your choice"

The other men walked back into the cell, and I pulled a lever separating them from the one subhuman I desired.

He looked upon me with unrivaled rage, yet I could see the fear in his eyes.

"Your choice"? I grind.

He slowly stuck the dome of his head between the bars and with great force I crashed the wooden club into his skull, and he fell quickly to the floor. I stuck the club between the bars and came down on him again to make sure he was unconscious before opening the cell door.

out cold he began to snore, and I quickly pulled him from the cell and secured the door behind me. double checking the lock and finally pulling the lever releasing the cattle back to full roam.

I smashed his hands with the heel of my boot making sure the bones broke before clubbing his kneecaps – assuring there would be no possibility of escape.

I grabbed his ankles and drug him down to the far end of the dungeon where the furnace was roaring, and I opened the door to his freedom.

"Father in heaven, take your servants sacrifice at your will oh Lord. May the strength of this subhuman glorify your name... Amen."

I clenched the hair and trousers of the young man and shoved him into the glowing flame. It was a matter of seconds before he revived into the brilliance of his fate. His dampened screams fading as the door closed on his life for good.

Silence fell throughout the chamber as I pulled the feed bucket from its hook and made my rounds.

****

"Why must you insist upon waking so early?" I barked.

Victoria was at my side and her newly found expression of love and passion was not my idea of a good morning.

"I found something…"

"Mmm?"

"Don't you wanna see what it is.

"No."

"Oh, I think you do."

I pulled my head from under my pillow to appease her silly games and hoped for a quick end to her shenanigans.

I was instantly adrenalized when I noticed a letter in her hand.

"Where did you get that" I snarled?

"Hey, calm down, it was just in that chest over there… we're married what's the big deal?"

"Did you…"

"Oh yeah, I read it… Estavon."

I had not heard my name spoken by another human in thirty-five years. I was unsure how to react. I felt the rage boiling in my blood and also the broken spirit of an innocent child crying from the depths of my soul.

"Why did you lie to me about your name... I think Estavon Is a wonderful name." she tried to reassure me of my emotions as I was unable to handle the situation properly. "Estavon and Victoria and baby Mark... unless we have a girl then I was thinking the name..."

"ENOUGH!! God does not permit women to be birthed of his will, you will not contaminate my castle with such blasphemous thoughts... hand me the letter now!"

She hurled the letter and envelope into my face and stormed out of the room.

I hadn't the heart to open the letter, it had been with me for decades and I just couldn't bear to read… but as it lay there on the bed, I couldn't help but finally satisfy my curiosity.

Dearest Estavon,

Due to the loss of your father in the war, I being too poor to care for you. I feel it to be in your best interest to be raised in the Kulsin monastery. I want you to know that I love you and will work as desperately as I can to gain enough financial security to get you back before long. A young man needs an education, especially in regards to Gods word. I know this is not what you would have but please understand the situation. It won't be long until we are together again, stay strong my son.

Your Loving Mother.

My heart shattered at her words; I cannot recall the last time I had truly wept, but I could no longer fight the tears. I sobbed with a fit of broken spirit unmatched in one's lifetime – if only for a moment.

I gathered my wits and a bottle of wine and made my way into the kitchen.

"Oh hey, so… I made you some breakfast, what do you think?"

"Thank you" I mumbled.

"Listen, I'm so sorry about your father I…"

"No" I waved, and she could see the emotion was too much. "I don't have a real memory of my father and my mother I haven't seen since I was 5 years old, it's ok."

"I just can't believe she sent you to Kulsin monastery, that place was horrible."

"What do you know of Kulsin?"

"I know it was full of people who tried to escape, and it burned to the ground."

"Or maybe someone burned it to the ground because of the people inside and we can thank God none escaped."

For an annoying young women, she caught on very quickly.

"You mean you… from what I heard they deserved it, course I wasn't born yet so I can only speculate fact from fiction… what was it really like in there?" she asked enthused.

"What is this in front of me, is it food?"

"It's oats and fruit… don't change the subject on me, you're not the only one who plays that game." She looked at me with an intense glare.

"Kulsin was …. "Well," I took a draw from my pipe and the smoke filled the atmosphere. "Kulsin was…"

"Go on"

I smashed my fists into my breakfast and stormed out of the kitchen. I cursed down the hallway and went up into the highest tower and locked the door behind me.

I pulled a rope from a chest tucked at the foot of a bed and slung it over a steel rod that protruded from the wall and tided It tightly to the rod at one end and fastened the other end tightly around my neck.

"Is this your desire oh Lord? Is this your will of me?"

I kicked the chair out from under me and my weight came down and I began to fight for air; my legs flailed and gasped in desperation for a breath; just as my eyes started to roll in the back of my skull, I caught the end of the bed post with my right foot and pulled the bed towards me for better control.

I loosened the knot and jumped down off the bed back to the stone floor and spent the rest of the day alone in prayer.

CHAPTER 5.

My God, the depravity of my mind – empty spirit is this who stares into the cold dark night, have I forsaken thee? Does thou relate in me twin of the Iscariot? My heart is numb Lord as the frozen winter nearing this land.

I kept on my side bound to the cold stone floor; eyes peering into the wall that lay before me. My body shook with the chill or the air and the shakes of a desperate need of drink. I allowed the thoughts to hold dominion and refused to fight back in any manner.

"Thy will be done oh Lord" I exhaled.

So weak my flesh that the desire to seek the warmth of the burning flame in the main chamber below did not seem a possibility by any stretch of the imagination.

"Estavon... Estavon" Victoria drew near.

I hadn't the will of interest.

"Estavon my God! Were you going to kill yourself?" She burst into the tower.

The noose still hung from the protruding rod above as she knelt at my side.

"I can see the rope marks on your neck poor thing... come to the main chamber, you are freezing cold, your lips are blue for God sake."

"Thou shall not take the name of the Lord thy God in vain." I faintly huffed.

"Yes, Yes... What on earth were you thinking, you are to be a Father and you're my husband, this is no way to react!"

She helped me to my feet, and we slowly made our way into the main chamber.

"... You know once when I was eleven, I fell from a tree and landed so hard it knocked the wind out of me, so I can relate to your pain."

I did not respond to her ludicrous sympathy. Here comparison meant as much to me as a subhuman begging for its life.

We reached the main chamber, and she plopped me into a chair near the fire and went off to fetch me some hot tea.

I stared into the flickering flames and imagined myself burning in the eternal fires of hell and I let out a gasp of fear and trembled in my chair.

"I beg for your mercy oh Lord!"

"Here is your tea... Why Estavon, you look frightened, like you've seen a ghost or something, are you alright?"

I could not release my hypnotic gaze, the glowing light of Satan had me in its spell and I was unable to utter a single syllable.

"I know what will cheer you up."

Vitoria began to disrobe and although attracted to her flesh I was yet unable to break my commitment to the flames.

Before she could touch me, I was out of the chair and started back out of the main chamber.

"What's wrong, don't you want me?"

"There are demons in this chamber, I can feel their presence." I gasped, lost in a sea of horrors.

"Well, we can go to our room, there's no demons in there I know for a fact."

"Yes, Yes… we must hurry!"

I ran at full speed, clutching the hand of Victoria and slammed the door behind us. When we got to our room, I slid a long rod of iron across the arms of the door and locked us safely inside.

"Blessed Father, I am grateful for the safety you've provided us from the evil one, Thank you Lord." I sighed in relief.

"Yes, thank God… So, are you ready for me?"

"NO!... This is not a night of sexual conquest."

"Conquest? I just was thinking like real quick and done, no conquesting necessary."

"Whore! Filthy Magdalen… Is it not enough that I must put up with gibberish at every waking hour… CONTROL YOURSELF!" I snapped.

Her eyes began to form tears, yet they did not fall. She tore deep into my soul and subdued my anger with a look, and I fell to my knees at her feet.

"Must we fight?" she gently spoke.

"Forgive me." I hushed.

"You know, I too feel the inner hell you speak of; The torturous voices of devils swaying me to lawlessness… where is your faith in the love of God Estavon?"

My worth was tarnished, I went back to the door with my face at the ground and crawled at the floor where I belonged. I faced the door and slipped out the iron rod barring us inside and I slithered my way to the worship chamber.

"ah ah," I wept "The women you have given me Father, I beg of you to allow her to cast no more stones upon me. I am not worthy of life… She calls me by a name and yet you call me nothing. What is her power oh Lord?" I looked up in silence.

At that moment it was as though the Lord put a clear message into my mind and wrote the answer in my heart.

I hurried back to the bedroom and broke the good news to Victoria.

"The Lord God has given unto me a message. So, clear I felt his words collect in my mind."

"And?" She looked in disbelief.

"Forgive my anger love, I am to teach you the way of life here in Ehpoe Forest, life in this castle… our home. We shall start new and grow in knowledge and strength together. For our walk with God and for our child to come."

"Oh Estavon." She wrapped her arms around me and held me as tight as the last time I saw my mother; my heart sang at the idea of a new start, and I kissed her lips prior to us making love as she so desired.

CHAPTER 6.

My body shivered in the pale light of the moon as the sweat poured from my sick skin. I tossed and I turned as though a demon embedded itself into my body involuntarily. The crawling bite forced me to scratch and claw at my flesh and I smashed my head into the frame of the bed and moaned in sorrowful agitation.

"Would you like me to fix you a drink? The pain will go away quickly I'm sure... my father had the same thing happen to him and as soon as he had a cup of wine the nightmares stopped."

"It is the Lords will that I suffer." I jerked.

"I just hate to see you in such a state... maybe I should take care of the animals in the lower chamber this day?"

"NO!" I made clear. "That is not a job fit for a woman, I will fulfil the Lords will even in sickness."

"Can I at least go see the animals?

I was unsure of Gods plan – did he want to burden Victoria with the hassle of cattle? Or should the duty of man remain in the eyes of man alone?

"When I recover from this illness, I will take you to see the animals."

"Deal" She clapped excitedly.

When the moon left, and the sun began to show, I forced my pathetic self from bed and made my way down to feed and water the cattle.

I took the wooden bucket from its hook and globed a pull of slop and made my rounds. I was slightly disoriented and very weak when I arrived at cell seventeen.

"Please…" A subhuman spoke at me. "I believe I am ill and will not recover, I do not wish to disturb you as you feed the rest… I just… I wish not to contaminate the area… may I be isolated from the rest of the prisoners?"

I would not lower myself to respond to a subhumans desire, but I could see sickness with which it spoke festering upon the skin.

I shuffled my way back to the entry door and just to the right – along with the other levers- I pulled and a small hole in each cell floor became exposed as I walked back to cell seventeen.

I pointed at the hole and the cattle understood that it was to enter. Hesitation began to spawn a degree of anger inside me, and I expressed that my patience was wearing thin. Slowly, the cattle sank down into the hole, when at once it disappeared for good.

I walked back over and pulled up the lever, closing the entry to the secondary furnace below.

"Anymore who are sick?" I yelled out.

I was met with silence, and I grabbed my bucket and continued with the feeding.

All the cells were rigged for such foreseen circumstance. I grabbed a bottle of cleaning formula of my own brewing and tossed it into cell seventeen and commanded the cattle to scrub their cell until the disease was eradicated.

As I fed, I could hear singing from cell twelve and the spiritual moan of slavery brought relief to my troubled morning – the blessed sound of subhuman suffering.

I finished up in the dungeon and walked the stairs up and made my way to the kitchen and was met halfway by Victoria.

"How are the animals doing?" she smiled.

"Well." I spoke unamused.

"You look slightly better this afternoon… I was thinking we could go on a walk if you're up for it?"

I decided fresh air near the stream may be good for detoxing; I gave her a nod of agreement and we dressed for the cold weather and walked our way to the water's edge.

"It will snow very soon, within a week I'm sure of it." I looked around.

"I like the snow, so beautiful in the trees and mountains."

"I suppose…" I mumbled.

I could see she wanted to get deep in an emotional conversation and I was just sick enough to entertain her foolishness.

"Do you ever get visitors – I mean is there any family that comes to the castle?"

"No visitors, just me."

"Oh" She looked at the ground disappointed. "Do you ever visit nearby villages or any community at all?"

"No… out of the question, I prefer solitude, which is why I live here."

"Were you always so grumpy?"

I shifted my eyes and figured I would always be interrogated unless I gave her something.

"Kulsin was made for mental torture and the crushing of one's soul. I was subject to every depravity you can imagine, weather physical or verbal. However - One evening, Father Albert believed he could have a go at me – he failed. I can withstand being beat and tortured by any means, but no man dare penetrate my flesh. I cut off his penis and forced him to eat it… I was eight years old. The Lord had given me the power to see into the future and I knew Alberts intentions; I sedated him by dropping a powder into his morning wine and carried out my rightful defense. While they were investigating his death, I secured most the entrance points prior and finished the remaining doors and set the place a blaze... no one survived, I knew I would succeed as the Lord assured me."

I could see she was saddened and uneasy but seemed to want more.

"There is no need for details, you must understand that what happens in life is for a reason, and that reason only God knows, we should not be broken by these things. I suffered greatly from the age of five when my mother gave me to Kulsin until the age of eight, a mere blip in time. I am forty years old now, the Lord has freed me from that hell long ago."

"I just heard so many stories and never met someone who was actually there, I can't imagine what you must have gone through."

"Well... it is over now, they paid for their sins, just like Sodom and Gomorrah before them." I grinned.

"Did you keep any diary from that time?"

"No diary, just prayers."

"Oh, I just wonder cause..."

"Why must you romanticize hell?" I looked into her eyes. "Somethings are better left to the imagination... God knows the reality and there is nothing romantic about torture I assure you... you dwell on devils when you should dwell on God."

She looked at the ground and I felt she understood my words finally – at least I wanted to believe so.

"You know enough of my torment, live with me now, in this very day, in this time... life is short I assure you."

"... I just want to know you, you're my husband."

"Know that I am a servant to the Lord God, a monk... a humble man... no more is inside of me." I assured.

I could see she was waiting for me to ask about her and although I dreaded the response I obliged.

"And what about you?"

"... Sometimes the past is better left to the imagination." She looked at me and smiled and I returned the sentiment.

"You know Estavon I don't know what love is, I've never experienced such a feeling but... whatever it is, I feel this is at least close to it?"

"I can agree." I smiled.

CHAPTER 7.

I felt my heartbeat – hands pressed upon my chest, the rhythm was off, and I attributed this to the lack of alcohol intake in the past two days; was this the case? For all I know my drunk heart could have been off for years now and I never would have noticed; either way I paid no mind and continued to dismember one of the fat cattle from cell three to fill the smoker. I used a sharp blade to debone the subhuman and I would toss the bone and scraps into cell one and the children had a feast worth clawing over. I collected the prime meat into sacks and hauled them off to the kitchen while Victoria was sleeping. I did not view butchering the weak a chore by any stretch, rather I enjoyed every hacking moment.

The apple wood smoked, and I shut the door tightly to allow the flavor to engulf the tender hanging loans. I tossed a freshly harvested brain into a pot and set it over flame; slicing in carrots, potatoes, celery, onion, and a verity of seasoning - My detoxified sweat leaked from my brow and fell dripping into the stew.

The last two days I have learned Gods expectation of being a good husband, so I attempted a more fancy setting for breakfast this morning.

"Victoria" I summed to eat.

I heard the clang of our bedroom door, and she made her way into the kitchen.

"Smells so good" She yawned.

"for you" I slid a bowl her way.

"Mmmm, so good," She slurped. "What is the meat in here, tastes amazing, but I can't say for sure what it is?"

"A cook never reveals his secrets."

She shook her head and continued to eat.

"Although I am still ill, I am thankful to still perform my tasks." I attempted small talk.

 "Nothing like hard work in the middle of the night I suppose." She joked. "Don't you ever sleep?

"Without my wine I fear I may never sleep properly again... but if it is the will of Lord so be it."

"Can you really hear the voice of God?"

"comes and goes."

"I pray sometimes but, I've never heard him speak... perhaps it is because I am a woman." She rolled her eyes in a playful manner.

"Perhaps," I tried to play along. "I find he speaks more when I am at my humblest suffering, I live in such a manner to invite more times of open communication."

"So, live like a miserable grump and you can talk with God... Got it" she mocked.

"The alternative is eternal damnation of ones soul in the burning fires of hell... I prefer to suffer on this earth now to secure eternity in the kingdom of Heaven."

"So, am I going to hell then? Cause I am happy, and no one will take that from me."

"What is happiness to you?"

"you know like... feeling good. like... the emotion of happy... that feeling."

"You test God for a feeling?"

"I just think if it feels good, it can't be a bad thing that's all... God created everything, so I mean happy is a thing."

"A feeling led Eve to eat the apple, a feeling led Cain to kill his brother and a feeling brought on the crucifixion of the Lord."

She did not respond but gave me a look of frustration.

"You may say, shall we not feel then… I say if you are truly with the Lord, you will know what it means to truly feel."

"If what you refer to as truly feeling means to act like you, no thanks."

"It is your freewill choice my dear."

"I choose to get another bowl of this food and hopefully get some sex after we eat."

My attempt at small talk was unsuccessful and I decided to try again another day.

"Estavon?"

"Yes?"

"May I send for a friend?"

"I don't understand?"

"My friend Samantha, from Berias?'

"No."

"Why not? She too wished to come here as well when I left, she was afraid her father would be upset so she stayed behind. "

"I did not send for you either. Anyone who finds this castle is permitted to by God and God alone."

She picked up her bowl and hurled it at me, splattering the content all over my robes before storming out of the room.

I did not understand her frustration given my hospitality. I cleaned her mess and made my way back to the dungeon.

I opened the door on cell three and drug out one of my fat cattle while he was momentarily sedated – then again drug out a muscular subhuman a few cells over and I locked them together in cell four. Twenty minutes had passed when they both finally started to come to.

"Now I command you." I ordered. "Fight to the death."

Both men stared into each other's eyes with a sense of fear and unwillingness to do harm to one another - had I not proposed a deal, I felt neither one would strike the other.

"The winner may set free anyone in this chamber, free from its cell indefinitely."

Upon hearing my words, I watched a course of adrenaline pump through both men and the fat one came in with his weight, smashing the muscular one into the cell bars. The more fit cattle gouged its fingers into the fat one's eyes and blood began to poor from them. With the advantage, the muscular subhuman forced the fat one to the ground and began to smash his skull repeatedly into the hard rock floor, until life left its body.

I stared without blinking into the violence; Neither adrenaline nor euphoria presented itself, I simply watched to watch.

"Choose whom you wish to set free from the cell." I welcomed.

"My son in cell one, his name is Adam, he has red hair, and his eyes are blue, please see to it that he is returned to Berias, his mother's name is Ann." He spoke rapidly in one breath… "Adam wait at the cell door for your release!" he cried.

I made my way down to cell one and I found a red-haired blue eyed subhuman waiting at his father request. The other children were motioned back and separated in the cell by a pull of a lever.

I ushered the boy out and his demeanor was calm and frightened. The urchin followed at my side as we stood face to face with his father at cell four.

His father quickly took him in his arms and began to promise his safe return to

Berias where his mother was waiting for him. As the cattle embraced, I pulled a long dagger from my robe and plunged it deep into the side of the boys neck and watched the blood spurt from the wound.

"FREEDOM!" I screamed.

The fathers cries echoed throughout the dungeon; yet again I merely performed an act and felt nothing worth wild.

The body fell to the ground and the father clasped tightly to the boy in hysterics.

I left the scene and nonchalantly made my way back to Victoria.

I peeked into the library chamber and saw Victoria in deep trance; lost in the pages of an imaginary world and decided to let her be, but as I turned to leave the dagger fell from my robe and clanged off the stone floor, setting her free from her stupor.

"Estavon, you startled me, what was that noise?" she asked.

"The cattle, I merely dropped the key to its... just a key, forgive me."

"Alright, I shall continue to read now, I'll be here if you need me."

"Enjoy your peace my dear." I smiled.

As she turned back into her book, I had the most peculiar feeling fall upon me. Ever so slowly, I crept my way over until I was just behind her. My shadow falling behind us and I slowed my breathing to faint sups. I watched as her chest rose up and down... up and down... I could hear the air fill her lungs and she was lost again in her own little world.

Nearly a full two minutes passed, and I remained. She was blindly unaware of my presence. I had no thought, no feeling nor emotion of any kind; I merely stared at her and no more than this.

Whenever so quietly… I stepped back and softly inched out of the room and headed down for the worship chamber for a quick chat with the Lord.

CHAPTER 8.

Monotony in abundance! – My God the words of a woman and the actions of a sober fool. My life became the small hand of a clock, dragging and spinning in the same laborious cycle. I awoke, I ate, fed cattle, and listened to the gibberish of a now twenty-year-old brat demand worthless adorations from me. My Father in heaven what has become of my quite life?

The moon showed through the single bedroom window and fell full on my wide-awake eyes. Her snoring resonated off the stone walls and sick feelings of emotion poured over me and I could bear it no more.

The presence of God had numbed to the point of nonexistence and his absence was forcing my nature to make itself truly known. For without the connection of the

Almighty I knew the devil seeks to corrupt. As to suffer like Job, I could only wish the Lord would then eradicate those humans near to me.

I rose from my bed and left the room, heading for my library chamber.

Upon arrival, I pulled a piece of parchment from a drawer and began to write my plea to the Lord God.

Merciful Father,

I beg thee oh Lord for thy embrace, wretched man I may be, I still desire to do thy will God. I am a simple Monk and though my words may not be written in proper form, I ask for your forgiveness Father. For what hath I done to grieve away thee? It is the woman you gave me Father; she has cursed me to the lake of fire, and I wish to retrieve my rib from her insides and cast her to the burning sulfur. Thee, thou, thy, thus and whatever you prefer God - know that I have felt more burden then I can bear... HELP ME!

I folded the parchment and carried it off to the worship room.

I placed it on the altar and lit it a flame and prayed for an answer in dark times.

These past nine months have been a nightmare - to put it gently, and I was nothing but alone in the matter. I unfolded my hands, straightened myself back to my feet and walked to the main chamber.

My eyes fell on the sparkling glass that bites like a snake and the serpent was calling to me. I reminisced of the days not long ago and recalled a time where I was in charge of time and all life beneath its mortal grasp. Anxiety forged its way through my desperate brain waves, and I was just about to break when...

"Is that what you want?" Victoria cut from the shadows.

"Perhaps." I mumbled.

"Go on then... Don't let me stop you." She taunted.

The devil gleamed inside me, and I reached for the bottle.

"Estavon, what is happening to me?"

I looked over and could see Victoria's water flowing out and she began to go into a panic, and I rushed over to help her onto the rug near the fire light.

"Baby, it's the baby, he's coming" she tightened her grip in my hand.

"Breath... no talking, just breath." I calmly assured.

With my free hand I pulled the bottle of wine from the shelf behind me and asked her to drink to relieve the pain; she quickly began to guzzle the content.

"More... GO GET MORE!" she screamed in pain, slamming the glass into the wall near us.

I ran into the kitchen and grabbed two full bottles and hurried back to her side.

"Here, drink." I remained calm, handing her the bottle and placing cushions under and around her for comfort.

"AAAHHHHH." She screamed as she pushed while sweat and tears befell her.

"Keep your breathing in check and keep pushing." I reminded her.

"YOU THINK!! Please make it stop, please!"

"Just keep pushing."

She screamed and insulted me for nearly an hour when finally, her body gave, and I could see a small child between her legs now nestled in the palm of my hands.

My joy quickly turning into horror.

"LUCIFER! THE SPAWN OF THE DEVIL!" I screamed into the castle.

"What is it, Estavon? Please hand me Mark."

"THIS CHILD IS THE MARK OF THE BEAST!!"

"What do you mean?" Victoria began to grow in intense fear.

"FEMALE!!, THE WORK OF DEVILS!" I cried, turning the child to her eyes, and reviling the sacrilege.

"It's ok Estavon, maybe God just…"

"NONSENSE, I WILL NOT HAVE YOUR WORDS DEFILE THIS CASTLE ANY FURTHER!"

In one quick motion I tossed the baby into the fireplace and held Victoria to the floor as the flames consumed the demon. Her piercing screams tore through my ears and the high frequency nearly burst my ear drums. She clawed and struck at me with every strength she could muster. We watched as the child returned to hell from whence it came.

I shoved off her and grabbed one of the bottles that hadn't been tipped over in the struggle and began downing the content with a ravenous thirst. She cursed my life and bawled her eyes into the flames as I made my way to the liquor cabinet.

"IS THIS YOUR WILL OH LORD?" I screamed, as I began to down every bottle, I could lay my hands on.

"AAAAAHHHHH"

Victoria let out a blood curdling scream as she plunged a knife into my side.

I smacked her to the floor and pulled the knife from my flesh and licked the blood till the blade shined clean.

"JEZEBELL!... YOU BIRTH SATAN INTO MY CASTLE, FROM MY FLESH AND INTO OUR HOME!"

"You bastard, you BASTARD!" she cried in her suffering.

I sent my fist into the side of her head as hard as I could rendering her unconscious. I grabbed her ankles and slid her down the main hall.

"Christ, this women is a whore, a mother of demons, Why does thou contaminate my castle, Lord?" I continued dragging her limp body. "See to it her seed be locked in the bottomless pit where it crawled from and never again let Satan's creatures free from their prison again oh Lord."

Her head bashed off every step as I drug her down into the dungeon where she belonged – with the rest of the subhumans.

The door to cell four flew open as I drug her inside her new dwelling. Her body flopped over bulging rock and stained blood as I left her pathetic form laying on the cold stone floor.

The door clanged shut and I made sure it was locked tightly and as I made my way out of the dungeon I screamed.

"There will be no food nor water for three days!"

CHAPTER 9.

A winter storm consumed the fallen leaves of Ehpoe Forest; violently it took over the landscape. I watched from the highest tower window and felt the same rage inside myself – emotions once more vanished without a trace. The storm lasted for all three days of isolated contemplation. I sat in a sea of unbridled vengeance and humility, neither moved nor broken. I did not speak with the lord, rather I grieved away his spirit, until inside me was nothing but silence.

Crackling from a small fire intertwined with the furry of an unhinged snow god, my heart did harden. I rose from my chair and fed the flames a few small rounds of wood and considered adding a mixture of death into my wine bottle. I returned to my chair and resumed my lost gaze into the vast takeover of endless white. Perhaps this is the only answer I may find in this solitary confinement?

"It is done." I announced and headed for the door.

One foot in front of another, I descended from the tower and down the main hall for the front door.

The freezing bite of winter hit my form and instantly chilled me to the bone. I walked into the harsh powder as it crystallized my beard and drenched my robes. I walked and walked and walked some more, until I came to a tree, I admired from the tower window and sat down at its base. The swirling blizzard made it near impossible to see a mere two feet. I closed my eyes and called for deaths embrace.

"Hello, Hello, you alright sir?"

A Voice cut into my drowning, and my eyes cracked open ever so slightly.

"By God, he's still alive."

I was numb from feeling and near death, when two men loaded me on a slay and hauled me back to the castle.

"Get him to the fire, hurry."

"I got his legs dad; you get his arms."

"1,2,3 LIFT"

The light hit faintly, and I closed my eyes until we reached the fireside.

"is he going to live dad?"

"I'm not sure, we can just thank God, we found him while we did."

"I'll feed the fire, maybe go make him soup? I'm sure there is a kitchen in this place somewhere."

"Keep an eye on him son, holler if you feel necessary."

I watched the man leave and the young boy stared into my eyes. My body was riddled in pain as I began to unthaw.

"Wine boy, wine" I barley breathed.

He looked about the room and retrieved my drink from the shelf near the door and he pressed it to my lips.

"Here you are sir, you must be in incredible pain."

I began to shiver ever so slightly and as I warmed the shivers grew increasingly.

"Here is some soup sir, just what I could find… carrots, potato, celery, onion, few dashes of season. Hope it tastes fine."

He handed me a bowl as he and his son began to eat their own portion.

"unbelievable sir, we are heading to Berias, and this damn storm came in. we got a little disoriented and when I thought I seen a faint light in the distance, if only for a second. We started our way towards it and seen this castle here. I noticed some footprints in the snow and decided we'd better check, in case someone got turned around in the mess. Glad we looked, you'd of never made it for sure."

"Dads a good tracker"

"Is it just you and the boy" I whispered – given my strength.

"Yeah, we are heading back from Elksgro, I had some business there and figured my boy could use a lesson in the family business."

"Dad makes hats from animal fur and sells them to big markets."

"Everything was going well until this damn storm blew in… I figured it was gonna come soon, so I prepared for it ahead of time. Never knew there was a castle out here, glad we stumbled on it."

I drank my wine, and the shivers began to slow, and I gathered a decent degree of strength.

"There are rumors of my home, none are true of course, I'm but a humble monk…

I was off fetching firewood when I got turned around, bless the Lord, you found me." I convinced them the now truth.

"Never heard any rumors, but we can agree on Gods hand in the matter… can I ask you something about monks? Always been curious?"

"Of course." I agreed, inwardly unamused.

"Do monks live in celibacy?"

I could see his inner perversion and I indulged his desire.

"Interested in women are you, well you came to the right castle."

His grin confirmed my suspicions, and I had the boy retrieve a special bottle of wine from the kitchen branded "ol'15."

"My best wine for your kind deeds." I offered.

"Thank you, sir... well son, it's a special occasion, don't tell your mother." It poured them both a glass.

"Why waste any more time, I feel my strength has sufficiently returned, shall we go meet the ladies?" I ushered them to the dungeon.

Their excitement was not lacking as I opened the door.

The cattle barked and begged for release, The smell from three days of neglect was horrendous.

"Pick your lady sir." I grinned.

The terror that held their expressions was to die for.

"What is this" the older one shuttered.

"This is what you dream of sir" I guided him down the cell block.

"Dad." The small one uttered.

"Be calm son, I'm sure we will understand…"

"All your desires fulfilled, and none need ever know." I cut in.

I could see the father considering my offer and his eyes seem to fall on a young blonde in cell eleven.

"Good choice sir, she can be all yours if you simply wish it true."

"I uh… I… I… I accept."

"Excellent, might I suggest the brunette for your boy?"

"Dad."

"That'll be fine yes." it confirmed.

I could see their eyes begin to weigh heavy, I watched as they began to fade slowly into unconsciousness.

"Hope you enjoyed ol'15, works great doesn't it." I smiled.

"Damn, you, sir." He huffed as they both fell wobbling to the floor.

The old man was heavy set and a good edition to cell three, while his boy was roughly fifteen and in good shape, I felt him fitting for cell nineteen.

After some lever pulls and dragging, I pulled the wooden bucket from its hook and began to make my rounds feeding the cattle.

As I dumped slop into cell four, I took a quick glance at the broken beauty I once loved; she did not speak or give any sign of emotion, instead she sat in her solitary cell lost in emptiness as I continued my rounds.

After my last dump of slop and return to the exit, I passed cell four and Victoria finally spoke.

"Estavon." Her gentle voice lured.

I did not respond but felt something stir inside me.

"You were right… I suffer here, now I hear the Lord speak to me – even to a woman if you can believe it true. His voice is so clear."

I looked at her with fascination and belief in her sincerity.

"I know what happened to you at Kulsin… it's what you're doing to us here, the Lord has shown me." she turned her eyes from the floor and peered into mine. "You claim you are doing Gods will but, I know you aim to be God… you will NEVER be God, you are no different than the men and women you have locked up in these cells and you know it." she hissed.

The hardening of my heart led me to feel no sympathy for her delusions. I simply returned the gaze and allowed her to express her psychotic ramblings like all the other times.

"You feel these words, yet you hide… pathetic… a monk of God well… I only see a cowardly child and no more."

She thought she could penetrate my calloused heart, but at the ending of her words I simply continued to the door and left without a second thought.

I walked the great hall and when to my surprise a young women stood at the entrance of the castle, just inside the doors.

CHAPTER 10.

"Hello… I'm sorry to enter without permission; I followed a man and his boy here… it's a long story."

She shivered and I escorted her to the fireside.

"Sorry again." She continued. "I just couldn't take the cold."

"No trouble." I assured. "Please tell your story."

"I'm looking for my friend Victoria, she searched for what I believe to be this place some time ago, I am Samantha… I heard this father talking to his son about heading back to Berias and I wanted to leave Elksgro so bad I figured maybe I would see this place upon my return, so I followed them. I was supposed to leave with her originally but was scared of what my father might do but, I no longer have those fears."

She's shown more beautiful then Victoria; dark black hair and emerald eyes, I was lost in her beauty that I faintly recalled her words.

"anyways, is Victoria here?"

"She is." I calmly presented and her excitement grew. "However, she is being cared for in the medical chamber, her trip here was not met without misfortune and we will not be taking visitation this evening… but if you wish to spend a night here and wait you are of course welcome?"

"I wish to see her first thing in the morning then." She firmly stated.

"Of course." I nodded. "We have a guest room available; might I interest you in some wine? It will help warm you up I'm certain."

"No thank you." She was leery and I could tell she was of greater intelligence than all who previously entered this castle.

"Victoria spoke a lot about you." I tried to ease her suspicions. "She had hoped you to come some time ago."

"I was waiting for my chance, when the opportunity presented, I took it."

"She was struck ill just a little over a week ago, a violent cough and slight traces of blood in her mucus... I believe however a full recovery will be met shortly."

"Who are you exactly?" she began to question.

"I am a simple monk."

She looked dissatisfied and on nerve. I tried to confront her obvious emotions.

"No need for worry my child, the Lord has permitted me to a life of kind service and chastity. Victoria has found a great deal of peace since living here, she was indeed like yourself when she arrived. I do not take offence I assure you, from what she described her life before here I understand the distrust." I smiled, yet I felt she wasn't buying it.

"Yes, well... I'm quite tired, I would like to end this night and see Victoria sooner rather than later."

"Of course, right this way."

I lead her to the guest chamber and shut her alone inside the room, locking it behind me, I headed down into the dungeon.

"Well Victoria, your dear friend Samantha has come for." I taunted.

"You bastard, you leave her alone!" she grit her teeth.

"No trust in your husband? Perhaps a new wife might be the solution?"

"I'll kill you I swear, I'LL KILL YOU!"

She pressed herself tightly to the cell bars as I figured she would. Quickly I reached my arm in and grabbed her by the throat and squeezed as hard as I could until she passed out cold.

I drug her from her cell and slung her over my shoulder, then carried her up the stairs and laid her in one of the rarely used guest rooms where I quickly made it up into a quarantine site.

I went over in my mind the dilemma of her possibly speaking and how I might make certain without a shadow of a doubt she would not come to during her visit with Samantha. I could only come to one sure resolution.

She must die.

I entered Samanthas room, and she was to my delight fast asleep -exhausted no doubt from her journey.

I crept to her bedside and placed a shackle on her wrist and attached the other end to the fixed bed post – likewise to her other arm. I slithered to the end of the bed and secured her feet as well.

Gently I slid up her dress and clenched my hand over her mouth as I began to penetrate her. She fought to no avail, and her squirms only made the act more pleasurable. After some minutes I emptied my seed inside her and left her screaming in tears.

"Dear God does the snow still fall." I prayed allowed. "Does thou still hear me Lord, I seek your forgiveness, your mighty wisdom Father... a mistake I made I now seek to rectify; the first women you sent Lord forgive my haste, I see now it was the second women whom you chose to bear the child." I began to feel the Holy Spirit enter. "Bless you Lord, I feel your presence now, never again shall I be led astray."

I crawled backwards out of the worship room and felt the relief one could only receive as a gift from a loving father.

"From this day forth I shall abstain from hard drink in preparation for the birth of my son; and adding to this I shall attempt the act of generosity when seen fit."

With the conclusion of my words, I headed back to the quarantine chamber where I sat with Victoria once more.

"Fool I am." I teared up. "You were not the vessel, but the motherly figure sent to raise the child, I see this now."

"Estavon." she spoke in a state of fragile come to.

"My dear, forgive my rage, forgive my wrath, and forgive my evil nature."

She rested her hand upon my shoulder and her tender touch moved to my cheek.

"I hate you!" she screeched as she tore her infectious nails into my skin, blood drizzling down my face.

I did not get upset, I did not restrain her, but allowed her rightfully gained fit to unfold upon me.

I was shoved from the bed and my skull smashed mightily on the rock floor and blood lightly pooled – conscious, I quickly rose to my feet and caught Vitoria before she escaped the chamber.

"I deserve your punishment, but you would be reminded I did not take your life or sell you out to strangers." I attempted to persuade.

She continued to fight – out of desperation I pulled her over to the pillory I had for just such an event and locked her inside to the tune of high-pitched screams.

"If you cannot control your temper, I shall have no choice but to leave you locked up."

She hurled a wad of spit into my face, and I grabbed the chain that hung from the device and pulled her from the room and into Samanthas chamber.

"Allow your friend to share the good news." I snarled.

I secured her to an iron loop at the foot of the wall near the bed and allowed them private conversation. Slamming the door, I tended to my wounds in the high tower with piece and quite.

My face had been beaten and clawed nearly to the point I was unrecognizable - I felt no anger as I deserved every blow. I rubbed what medicine I had crafted some time ago and hoped it was still potent enough to cure. I contemplated the future and new the impossibility of gaining Victorias trust and I knew not what I could do. I had nine months to make amends and I prayed to the Lord it was time enough to fix all my mistakes.

CHAPTER 11.

I chopped a fresh chunk of cattle in the kitchen chamber, the fatty meat was of the highest quality – I figured the only way to make amends would be to start off the day with a good meal. I had prayed all night for the Lord to impress upon their hearts that I would be a good husband and father from this day forth.

I dished up three potions of soup and made my way down the hall.

"AAAAHHHH." Screams of terror startled me - so that the bowls of soup crashed to the stone floor.

I hurried to the guest chamber and was met with a crushing reality.

"She'd dead, she's dead!" Samantha sobbed.

I rushed to her side and the grim truth of these words sank into the depths of my soul – it was all so very real.

"Victoria" I whispered, fighting my sorrow, and clenching her hand; still locked in the pillory.

"This is your fault, you sick bastard!" Samantha hurled her insults with bitter rage.

"Victoria" I continued, hoping by the miracle of God she would hear my voice and wake.

Her skin was cold to the touch, suggesting she went sometime in the night. I released her from her prison and carried her gently by the fireside. It was as if I could hear her persistent ramblings as clear as day. I could see the torture of her spirit as she watched her child feed the flames. I can see now her withered frame and broken innocents of a life lived with me – Oh Lord what a wretched man I am.

"You bastard, AAAHHHH" Samantha resumed her hatred.

"Lord God in heaven, I offer to you a woman - Of which I have never known another alike. Your Gift to this horrible earth and I the serpent who betrayed your precious creation. Forgive me for my short comings and I beg thee, do not condemn this woman for my actions Father. She is offered to be at your side, look at her heart Father and cast out mine. As you received her child, so shall you receive her. My love... Victoria."

I gently let go of her lifeless body and she fell into the fire. As I watched the child burn, so too did I look upon the flesh of my wife. Skin peeled and exposed meat, quickly revealing the bone. The black bubbling and stench of burning flesh and hair was strong – as was her will.

"NNOOOOOO, NOOO!" Samantha screamed in agony.

I had spent the small portion of tears I could possibly offer and reached for a bottle of wine that sat on a shelf near the fireplace.

"The will of the Lord." I breathed.

I laid in the bed next to Samantha and watched as she tried with all her strength to escape her shackles. Gently I would stretch my hand and wipe away every tear that fell upon her cheek. I was lost for words and lost for emotion; I simply laid there, watched her pain, and imagined the release of my own.

After long intervals of emotional outburst, Samantha finally collapsed from exhaustion.

"My God, let this woman not be shaken by death nor let her fear life. The time we have together Lord, let it be fruitful – if it be your will."

I fished out the remaining bones and pile of ash left from Victoria and placed them in a trunk and decided to store them safely in the high tower. I lifted the small trunk and headed out of the room and up the stairs.

"Mmmmmmmm mmmm." I hummed a somber tune as I entered the high tower chamber.

"God, I pray to thee again, let this woman rest in your arms and welcome her home."

I placed the trunk in the dark side of the cylindrical room and sat on the bed staring at its melancholy.

"She's gone." Reality again hit and I was once more crushed.

I took a blade from the bedside drawer and began carving her name into the flesh of my arm. The pain was welcomed as I continued to swig my wine.

"Madness, madness Father is near, I beg you do not let me succumb to its nature." I lay staring into the ceiling of the dark room. "Does not the sun reach this side of the castle." I cursed. "FATHER!" I spit in deep grievance. "FATHER! FATHER! FATHER!" I sobbed with great intensity.

I awoke in severe depression, my head spun, and ached, empty bottles and broken glass decorated my bed – instantly reflecting upon the loss of my true love. The stars shown from my window and the moonlight passed through the single connection to the outside and I walked over and peered into a sea of white.

"Curse this winter Lord" I muttered.

As I reached out to the cabinet behind me for a bottle, I was disappointed in finding it empty.

I wobbled down the stairs and opened the door to the guest room to check on Samantha.

Eyes fixed at the ceiling above and riding a wave of depression all her own. I decided to free her hands and allow her some much-needed circulation.

"Calm... I'm in no mood." I hiccupped.

"I'm hungry." She sweetly stated.

"... I'll get you something."

I stumbled out of the room and went for the kitchen.

I pulled a slab of meat from the smoker and grabbed an apple and hurried back to her.

"Here eat."

"What meat is this? It's not of an animal."

"It's meat is it not... eat it."

"What is it?" she demanded, annoyingly.

"From my best cattle I assure you."

"You mean there is people here beside us?"

"People?" I acted confused.

"This is human." She threw the meat into my face.

"Well, Try some… you may like it, never know till you…BBBRRRRppp."

"You are a disgrace, you're disgusting and vile and if you do not free me now, I swear to you I will pound my stomach and kill this demon that grows inside of me."

I smacked her in the face, and she flew back onto the bed, and I secured her shackles once more.

"Why do you reject my kindness…CAN I NOT BE KIND?

"NEVER, you are weak, degenerate pig and you do not speak with the Lord but speak with the Devil."

"EEENNNOOOUUUGGGHHHHH!"

I climbed on top of her and tore her dress from her body and began to insert myself inside her once more.

"SEEXXX, IS THIS ALL YOU CARE ABOUT SEEXXX!!" I screamed.

She rattled and spit and tried to bite at my flesh and I choked her until she would nearly faint and release the air back inside of her at the last moments before black out.

"HAHAHAHAHAHA" I laughed in madness.

"If it be Gods will, Gods will, Gods will, Gods will." I jeered repeatedly.

I finally released my seed again and spit in her face upon discharge and rolled from her to the floor and laughed in hysterics.

"AAAAHHHHH" Samantha cried out in anguish.

"LORD AM I NOT A DOG, A FOOL OR AM I NOT SPOKEN TO BY SATAN THEN

LORD?" hahahaha. "DA DA, DADA, DA, DA, DA, DADADA…" HAHAHAHA.

I had reached the pinnacle of madness; I felt a total loss of control – motor skills and emotion in the hands of demons.

"FOOL, Coward, wretched man!" Samantha hissed.

"FOOL, COWARD, WRETCHED MAN!" I mocked. "You know nothing of our live – that of Victorias love, for her home, for this place, for me."

"She could never love you!" she yelled.

"She came here of her own free will and we were married by her free will, and she had the audacity to bare a demon. Before the child we had a fairy tale life, of which you could only dream."

"LIES!!! YOU LIAR!!"

"Now she is gone forever! And time stops for no man hahahahaha, ash's, to ash's hahahaha. I shall celebrate her memory, and you shall join me, as the mother of Gods future prophet."

"FUCK OFF!"

"Come now, we must prepare for the ball."

With minute sensibility -graced upon me no doubt by the Lord; I forced Samantha into Victorias pillory and made way for the dungeon.

"VIEW THEE, THE CATTLE OF GOD, THE SUB-HUMAN FILTH." I bellowed.

"My God." Samantha gasped.

"Who wishes to honor the memory of the queen of this castle?" I clowned.

"This is grotesque, surely you must free these people.

"CASTLE GROTESQUE!... for the love of the queen!"

I walked down the cells dancing and screaming perversions – I drug Samantha down with me.

"You there." I pointed to a strapping gentleman in cell eight. "Please do the honor of being our sacrifice, sacrifice, sacrifice…"

"YOU'RE MAD!"

I clubbed the man in the head, and he collapsed at the bars.

"BACK YOU SWINE, I COMMAND YOU, BACK!"

The rest of the cattle were locked in separate, and I pulled the man from his cell and dragged him over to the furnace.

"IS THIS ENOUGH FOR MY LOVE?"

"PLEASE, ENOUGH!" Samantha pleaded for me to stop.

I pulled a hatchet from my robes and began to hack chunks off the man and toss them about the chamber. Samanthas screams and the echoing choir of the cattle set the scene. Chunks were eaten by the desperate and the stomach popped releasing a foul odder into the chaotic air. I hacked and mutilated the corpse until it was a mere smear in the rock floor.

"NOT GOOD ENOUGH THEN?"

I pulled a child from cell one and tossed its feeble frame into the furnace.

"IS THIS SUFFICENT LORD?"

"Ppplease." Samantha begged.

"HAHAHAHAHA" I howled as the flames roared high.

"God please!" Samantha broke.

"God please!" I mocked.

I wiped my bloody hands across her face and pulled her dress up and had my way with her in front of God and cattle.

The subhumans lost their song and I felt every eye fall away. They retreated back into their cells and faced away and I was furious with their betrayal.

"WATCH!!! I COMMAND YOU!!" I shouted.

None did turn back to my attention - I pulled out of Samantha and made my way to the stairs.

"THEN SUFFER!" I screamed. Shutting the lights off and slamming the door shut, leaving the cattle in absolute darkness.

CHAPTER 12.

Alone – the silence was immense, and I sat glaring at the trunk containing Victorias remains.

"What does thou require for her return Father? I may offer you a life for a life; neither the innocents of a child nor health of a grown man seems to pay the debt. Why torture your servant, Lord?'

I picked up the trunk and tossed it out the window.

"AM I TO FORGET?" I cried.

The trunk disappeared into the deep snow as did the overwhelming sense of madness that befell me.

"I am tired Father." I declared – falling into my bed. "So tired."

Knock, Knock

My head pounding in violent torment and frame so weak I could hardly stand. I twisted my robes back into presentable order and cussed my way to the door.

"What demon does thou present to me this time." I cursed.

I opened the door and two small children stood before me. one boy and one girl, well kempt, beautiful, and handsome.

"What is your desire here?" I asked.

Neither child spoke a word but stared at me without the blinking of eyes.

My mouth fell ever so slightly, as I studied the children with a paranoid eye.

Freezing, blistering cold outside – and neither child looked to have been touched by the winter chill; Dry and rosy, calm, and collected they stood still. Neither did their chest lift for intake, nor fall with exhalation. I figure they were twins, both reflecting similar features. Pale eyes, black hair, and sturdy jaws; the girl in a thin white gown and the boy in common black attire. But it was the long-drawn emptiness they held in their eyes that was most familiar.

"What is your desire here?" I repeated.

Neither answered.

I ushered them inside and they took direction.

"Can I fix you something to eat?"

Neither answered.

I figured their age roughly to be about eleven years old; both walking with the same stride as the other.

"Are your parents near?" I asked.

Neither answered.

I sat them both at the table and began to fix a meal, I frequently would glance over to see if either one would make a move.

Through the entire preparation, neither one blinked nor moved a muscle whatsoever.

"I can understand silence," I tried to connect. "with all that has gone on in this castle as of late, silence is a blessing no doubt."

Zero reaction.

I dished their plates and tossed them in front of their face to see if they would startle.

Nothing.

As I gazed upon them, I noticed the boy motioning me to follow him yet... he did not move in the slightest.

"Go on then." I agreed.

The girl remained seated, but the boy rose from his chair, and I followed him out of the kitchen and down the hall.

When we arrived at the dungeon, I was hesitant to allow entry, but it was as if I could feel his persistence demanding we enter.

I turned the key and the door opened. I pulled a lever and allowed light to shine once more into the chamber. Moans and gasps at the bright light filled the putrid air.

The boy walked down the cell block and I followed, when he stopped just shy of Samanatha who was facing the wall ahead.

"Well Samantha, have we learned our…"

I turned the pillory and found Samantha cold and lifeless.

I spun and locked eyes with the child who held a soulless gaze upon me.

"What is this?" I barked.

He did not react.

I was confused – unsure how to act, I felt an odd sense of desperation to wake from what I was sure was a dream…

"Lord! What dark magic is this?" I called out to the heavens. "Is this your idea of a game Father?"

The child seemed to speak but I could not make out the cacophony of voices that merely crowded the inner structures of my mind.

"Does this please you?" I asked.

I released her from her shackles and carried her body to the furnace.

"Thy will be done."

I tossed her into the slow burning flames and shut the door tightly behind me.

I grabbed the wooden bucket from its hook and began to feed and water the cattle. Once completed I cleaned the floor - free of blood and chunks, and the dungeon was brought back to good running order.

"Thank you, Lord, for the opportunity to work and provide health for others." I praised.

Empty shell of a man – I marched back to the kitchen and the boy found his seat with the girl and I looked upon them with fascination.

"Why have you come here?" I tried. "Has the lord felt betrayed once more? Is this my punishment? ANSWER ME!"

Nothing.

I was nearly about to explode with rage when they both started to move ever so slowly. In unison, they reached into their pockets and pulled out a razor blade – I watched in awe. In a swift motion they both sliced open their wrists and blood flowed down to the floor and pooled around the feet of the chairs.

Their eyes did not fade, their hands did not tremble – as they were there they were gone.

"I do not understand your intent, Father?" I hid my face. "Are they children of Demons or are they yours sent?"

I started to cough uncontrollably, and blood hacked from my inner lungs, and I fell to the floor.

"If it is my time Father, know that I have served thee." I cried.

I shut my eyes and remained on the kitchen floor until I managed to settle my delusional mind and affirm my sins had been forgiven.

"Death Father? Am I only to taste death? All I love gone before me. Never to have a mother nor a wife; have I not tasted enough death in my life God? What am I to confront? Shall I lay broken, or shall I rise? Does either have a point?"

I managed to summarize my life in that moment defeated on the floor and realized it had been forty years of mere darkness.

"If it be thy will, Father." I uttered as I rose to my feet and headed for the library chamber.

I pulled from my books a map of the area and declared.

"For when the sun rises longest in the sky and the snow drowns to the core of the earth, I shall leave this place for good!"

CHAPTER 13.

Weeks had passed in the most dreadful detox. I convulsed in sweat and scratched in desperation – my mind fixated on the memory of Victoria and the brevity in which we spent our time together. As the demon of drink seeped from vain and passed through my skin, I began to clearly rationalize the loss and the enormity of sorrow that held me prisoner.

"Father had I known... WHAT A BASTARD I AM! My heart had been made into a character -referred to by many as evil - in my childhoods hour. I never knew my mother deeply; God help me Kulsin was hell... My name father is Damien Uriah Estavon, bestowed upon me at birth and as my mother tried to erase for my sake, I also hid from my love – I am a vile man. In the words of Samantha this Castle Grotesque shall one day be a forgotten ruin. I beg you

Lord before I leave my home, in the simplest of words – may my love return?"

Upon newly emerged suspicions, I rose to my feet and marched out of the castle.

The biting cold began to nip at every exposed area it could teeth as soon as I entered the frozen landscape. No storm did rage; I trudged through the waist high snow until I reached the bottom of the high tower window. I began to claw at the snow and searched for the remains of my love – hoping they lay intact inside the sturdy trunk.

After five minutes of digging, I finally caught the black trunks corner, and with a boost in adrenaline I clawed with anxious anticipation.

I heaved with both hands clasped to the handle and pulled the trunk free of the heavy snow.

Back inside the castle, I warmed myself with the trunk in the main chamber.

I had a vision in mind that I would place the remains in proper order -as available – in the worship room, I hoped with desperate and honest prayer, the Lord would restore my love to her original life. I felt so certain inside of my plan that, by faith alone, I believed God could deny me no request.

Once comfortable, I entered the worship room and began the ceremony.

"Father, I Damien Uriah Estavon come to you with a humble spirit, a monk, a man who now assumes the name he earned at birth. For once I was lost, but now am found. You have restored me to my proper place Father and now I come to you in hopes you will restore another. Though my mother tried to forgot my name, I know you have it written in the book of life. Father? My love is with you, my sweet Victoria, I beg you with all devotion in my heart, that you return her to this castle for which she so desires to be Lord. I have set the dust remains, and the bones of her structure in thy presence. For thou maketh man in thy image oh Lord, So shall thee make return my Love, Victoria. Amen."

Knock Knock

"If it be the children Lord - I assume thy servants - please see to it they move along their way."

Knock Knock

"My God, in desperate repentance, I beg thee to let this burden pass and that thou will restore my regret so that it may be altered."

Knock Knock

"THY WILL... BE DONE...LORD!"

I arrived at the front door and knew I would be met by the children; I did not wish their intervention at this time, but knew the Lord demanded it, I could not argue his will.

"What is your desire here." I gently welcomed.

To my bewilderment, only the boy was standing before me. Although, this time his appearance was more decomposed then prior meetings.

"What is your desire here?" I repeated in the same tone.

Once more he did not speak nor give any signal of his emotion.

I was in a better frame of mind in this particular meeting and decided to entertain the boy in a new manner - which I had been reluctant to try in my drunk stupor in times before.

I steered the boy down the hall and had him join me in the library for a more formal setting.

"I assume you have been sent here by the Lord, Pleased do sit…" I pulled him a chair near to mine – he sat. "My name is Damien Estavon, I am a monk here in Ehpoe Forest, I am pleased to make your acquaintance, I'm sure. The matter in which you are here is a simple one really, you see my wife Victoria had passed due to infection of the lung, and the Lord has no doubt sent you here for me to plead my case. I want to assure you that I cared for my wife dearly and although at times our relationship could be… oh how would you say – tumultuous. It is with undoubted certainty, that Victoria herself would demand return." He neither blinked nor flinched in the slightest as I carried on. "I can see I'm not making myself clear enough for you, uh, may I get you a drink or something?" He remained motionless and silent. "Yes, of course... um, where was I? oh yes... allow me to delve deeper if I may, you see... My life has been very uncomfortable to say the least and during the time Victoria was here, although loud and bratish, quite simply, I did adore her passions and desires and her knowledge of... well, you see there it is, I cannot honestly say I relate but." I began to grow anxious and sweat ever so slightly. "If all honesty must be brought forth, I must confess well..." I knew I had been found out and if it was the only way then so be it. "ALRIGHT! So, I did not know her nor her me on a deep level, I cannot say we shared common interest, there, are you satisfide then?" I flailed in my seat. "Damn it boy, what must I understand? What must I muster? How can I convince you I was indeed in love?" I begged.

The boy stared into an empty fixation, I finally realized he wasn't even looking into my eyes, but through them.

"Surly thou cannot be sent by the Lord?" I trembled slightly. "Do I then converse with a demon?"

The boy gave the most perverse grin – slightly turned and vanished before my very eyes.

I ran, with all the fear and energy left in me, I locked myself inside the worship room and begged the Lord for answers.

"Father." I panicked. "The devil is in my dwellings; I beg you Father never allow his return."

I fell to my knees and knew that my attempt to bring Victoria back into this world would be a far and away dream. I decided it best to hide myself from the world once more and allow my conversations with the Lord a break.

"Father I shall remain silent and absent from your presence for an extended time and allow our bond to strength before I fall any deeper in agony."

I rose to my feet and withdrew from the worship chamber. slowly and in extraordinary defeat, I slugged my way to the high tower and cursed the night of my conviction.

The day would fall in the same repetitive manner and the night would welcome my loneliness for the remainder of this cruel winter.

CHAPTER 14.

Dearest love Victoria,

I have kept my full name from your ears and hid my deepest emotions from your heart. My full name is, Damien Uriah Estavon, I am an abused monk from the demented walls of Kulsin Monastery where I had experienced torture of the most perverse kind. Beaten, starved, and locked in a small cell; however, the story of me killing and burning down the prison was true as I would have not tolerated penetration by no means. I have no desire in reliving these events, nor wish to write them in exact detail but will then list several examples for your imagination, so as to bring you clarity of sorts.

- Physical abuse with fists and objects
- Forced cannibalism
- Rape of others in plain view
- Drinking of urine in desperation
- Starvation for up to one week
- Infectious skin and sores
- Darkness and hard floor
- Sexual abuse of the verbal sort
- Theft and intolerable cell mates
- Desperation with most gruesome result

Now you may understand my life, by knowing all these.

things happened in frequent abundance to me for years.

I wadded up the letter and threw it into the fireplace. To ashamed to concluded with "your love, Damien" for what love was in me? I was a dog who urinates on the floor from beaten fear.

I walked to my window and beheld the melted snow under an inviting sun.

"In one weeks,' time, I shall leave this castle for good."

I turned back to the flames and watched the now black page flake to ash and soon vanish to the heavens to be with my love.

I left the high tower room and slowly roamed every inch of the castle – aside from the worship chamber – and took in many years of memories made. I dwelled on the passing of time and how quickly you grow old without even noticing, had you not stopped to realize it.

After my perusal, I started about the place packing important items I may need for my trip and headed to the library for examination of my escape route.

Over the past several months I have read and now decided to begin a new life on a ship, sailing the vast seas and take up the art of fishing. I had read many tales of the great waters and decided the endless view of sea and sky was the correct way to end my troubled life. according to my map - I nabbed from the Father and son duo prior to Samanthas arrival, there was a dock due north of Ehpoe showing it eighty-two miles away. I figured if I got tired of the sea, if the ship ever landed in a beautiful island somewhere, who dare stop me from staying.

I gathered up all I would carry on my trip and placed the baggage by the front door for quick departure, but as I turned from the door...

Knock knock

A jolt of unexpected fear hit me, but I knew this knock was slightly different than that of the child's, so I composed myself in calm manner and opened the door.

There before my eyes was an old women, roughly aged eighty-five and her eyes like that of the children -lifeless and long drawn.

"What is your desire here?" I asked in a cautious utterance.

She reached out her hand for mine and, though the fear of her not speaking erected the hair on my neck, I reached out and took her hand.

She led me at a snail's pace through the castle and down to the dungeon door. though she never dare speak, I understood her directions.

I opened the door, and she escorted me to cell twenty-five, the last cell on the block. Pointing her finger at the horror that lay inside.

Where once held eight of my young beautiful female cattle, now a decomposed muddle of black rot. The putrid stench invaded my nostrils and I gagged at its intolerable odder. The thick liquid oozed from the center and seeped just outside the cell and into the hall. I turned to check the health of the other cattle, and all was in perfect order.

"What Dark magic do you perform in my castle?"

I spun in circles, for the old women I aimed to confront was no longer present.

Normally I would call on the Lord in such occasions, but I kept the silence I agreed upon and instead forced a nonreaction and simply cleaned the vile matter.

The liquid clotted and tightened as I attempted to scrape it from the floor as if it were a living organism being harassed. I spent the remainder of the day wrestling it from its nest and withdrew to the sanitation chamber for deeper cleaning of my flesh.

I wish to say the night was more kind to me but another knock at the door called.

Knock knock

Knock knock

Knock knock

I tore from my chamber and cursed my way to the door and pulled open with force.

"Estavon"

"Victoria?" my eyes began to swell with blissful tears at my disbelief.

"Estavon." Her voice comforted.

I took her in my arms and held her with full adoration for some time.

"I received your letter you sent me, my sweet Damien, how dare you keep your name from me, such a handsome name, oh I must tell you what heaven is like, it is wonderful Damien, streets of gold, gates of pearl and jewel.”

Her lung power intact and her incessant need to ramble in full swing, my love was home.

“Yes, yes,” I cut in. “Victoria, in due time, allow me now to thank the Lord for your return, for the silence I’ve experience over the last several months has been excruciating. Please, please, come to the main chamber, let us sit by the fire side.”

We strolled happily into the castle and down the hall to the main chamber, I held her tightly in my arms.

I placed her in the chair across from mine and as I turned and sat in my chair… my eyes beheld and empty room.

I fell to my knees at once and begged the scenario untrue.

"FATHER, I BEG YOU, HER RETURN." I cried in desperation. "Please Father…" I began to trail my words, knowing the sound of silence all too well.

I smashed my fists into the stone floor and buried my face to the ground. I cried and then cried some more until exhaustion won the better of me and I finally collapsed from the fatigue.

Knock knock

I woke and ran to the front door and flung it open and there again was my love.

"Damien, look at the stars above, such a beautiful night to sit outside and gaze into the sky, don't you agree?"

"Oh course, let us sit together here on the porch and observe the stars." I pleaded with my inner mind that she does not vanish – I kept my eyes on her at all times.

"You see that star their Damien" She pointed.

"Yes, I see it, yes." I answered, Keeping my eyes on her.

"That's where I live, words cannot describe its beauty. Have you ever thought of what heaven looks like?"

"Oh yes, frequently" I assured.

"I could never imagine while on this earth such a place, I could only imagine Berias and this castle here - as the barriers allow one to possibly envision... I have broken free of this of course but, had I known I could leave sooner rather than later."

"Couldn't we all be so lucky." I smiled; my heart warm at her side.

"For the life of me, I cannot recall my death, I'm not even aware if I truly am dead or not but... I know since I am living in heaven, I must be... can you help me answer this, Damien?"

I gave a quick cough and stumbled through my response. "Well, you, you, um, well it was quite simple, unfortunately, you, um, well… you see, you had a lung infection and it just won in the end, you see, it was incurable really, there was nothing I could do for you, although of course I tried everything I could, naturally." I swayed.

"I see, a lung infection… no matter, I'm in a better place and that's what matters."

"Yes, yes, precisely" I confirmed. "um, Victoria."

"Yes?"

"can you help me now with a question, I wish to understand how you may stay here, permanently, is this possible for you?" I spoke fast so as not to be interrupted.

"Mmmm, I think so."

"Alright," I wasn't satisfied. "is there any chance you could arrive towards a definite, conclusion... maybe?"

"Mmmm, well why do I need to stay here, why don't you come with me, I mean it's far more beautiful up there then it is down here? Oh, I have to tell you about my dog, he's so cute, he."

"Yes, yes, lovely dog, now understand please, I cannot go there when I am sorely needed here, you understand, but if you are here then we can be together always like old times."

"if your sorely needed her, why are you packed to leave?" she caught me.

"Oh, no, no, no, I was not packed to leave, I was simply cleaning up for the coming summer, just making the castle more full." I trailed off.

I could see in my peripherals that the sun was beginning to rise and as the gentle pink caressed the far land, I noticed a change in Victoria.

"Damien, although I cannot fully grasp my being here in an expressed way, I do feel the rising sun spawns a call in me to leave for home."

"Victoria you must resist the urge I beg you, look." I turned to view the sunrise with her. "The sun has not yet fully risen.

I turned back and she was gone.

CHAPTER 15.

I awoke on the porch, chilled yet not terrible. I yawned and stretched and when my eyes did finally open; there at the arm of the steps, sat the boy.

"What is your desire here?" I asked agitated by his presence.

He as always gave me nothing.

I had seen the boy off and on for the past several month, he never hurt me nor attempted any unwanted shenanigans, he merely just watched me about the castle.

"Look I have just woke from outside, and it is already midday, I plan to bath and eat, nothing more." I tried to shoo him away.

He just stared as usual.

"Would you like a show? Do you desire entertainment? What is your poison then? Hmm..."

I must have struck a nerve for the second time, as a cacophony of voices rattled incoherently in my mind, and I assumed it to be the boys "YES" response.

"Well then, follow me." I beckoned.

I led the boy down into the dungeon hoping to scare him away for good.

"Here, you see, subhuman species, pathetic are they not?" I showcased.

I led him down the aisle and showed him all the cattle I had collected over the years, but when we got to cell twenty-four.

"The dark magic... curse you damn, spawn of Satan!" I went to attack the child, but he had vanished.

Inside the cell, lay ten corpses, crisscrossed, and mounded upon one another. The flies gathered in mass and the smell was less repulsive than the last, yet the rotting process had begun.

I retrieved the wheelbarrow near the entrance doors and began to haul the bodies, one by one to the furnace.

The cattle lost was that of my fattening stock. I knew that my meat supply would take a future hit given this loss and decided before more dark magic fell upon me, it would be best to start smoking some of my fat cattle in case of more unsolicited death.

After furnacing the bodies, I selected two scrumptiously plump fatties from cell seventeen, once wrangling them into shackles the boy appeared once more.

"Enough of your magic!" I shouted. "Allow me to pass, this is my food, you can have none of it!" I spat.

But the boy for a second time finally gave a motion. Extending his finger to a beauty in cell eighteen, I understood his perverse desire.

"Interesting, I have never allowed such conduct in my dungeon." I grinned. "You have a sick little mind you know."

The woman was locked alone - for I used her many times for my pleasure, and she was gorgeous to say the least.

I opened the cell door with her already sat in the far-left corner of the cell; I shoved the fatties inside and locked the three together - unlocking the fatties chains from the outside I commanded them.

"Have your way with her or die!"

They did not hesitate, hell, one could say no command was needed. They pinned her down in the center of the floor and tore her dress from her body. My eyes fell on the boy and his blinkless stare fixed upon the obscenity. I could see he was engaged in the act but something inside me indicated the boy was not satisfide in any readable measure. I was put off with his empty pleasure meter and looked on as the fatties weight crushed the small female.

"Your desires fall short – as do mine." I understood. "The reality is never as pleasing as the thought, am I wrong?" I looked at the boy for acknowledgement.

Nothing.

"I don't need words to gather your answer, no... I quite understand, if not more so with silence."

When the fatties had accomplished their pleasure, I pulled a crossbow from the entrance shelf and put them down.

"Give me a hand with the butchering and I'll make you a fine meal boy."

But as usual when the work began so did the disappearing act.

I spent the day getting the fatties deboned and hung in the smoker. When night fell, a desired wish came true.

Knock knock

"Damien."

"Victoria." I embraced her tightly.

"The stars shine brighter this night do they not?"

I agreed and kept my eyes on her as always.

"Mark, said you put on a marvelous show for him this afternoon, please tell me the story." She looked on with excitement.

I was overcome with horror. "Mark?" I trembled.

"Yes, Mark, he said you both have spent a little time together; I don't mind if you do, Samantha is my friend and you're the boy's father after all, honestly it is ok."

I could feel the demonic plague of a panic attack begin to bubble in my veins and race into my skull. The boy exists, that must have made the other girl…

"I am sorry Mary Ann does not wish to join in play, she is awful shy and believes you do not want her here, I tried speaking with her but…"

Her words fell upon def ears. I was lost in the grim reality that my children born of Samantha still roam this earth… but what then of…

"Victoria, please" I interrupted her before the panic attack could take full charge. "The female child you birthed, the one that I…" I was unable to finish, for the devilish act I performed ran clear in my mind.

"It's ok, Lilith does not hold any grudge, she wishes to meet you, but she is currently on probation from this realm. She should be free for a visit shortly… oh and as for

Samantha, well she just, we don't really talk much, she hangs out with a different crowed I just don't connect with so… yeah."

Victorias typical demeanor was making the panic rise more potent inside of me, so much so I jolted to my feet, ran into the castle, and made my way to the high tower without looking back.

I kicked open the door to the worship chamber and fell to my knees.

"Silence be broken Lord! I cannot contain the devil that runs rampant in my brain any longer. The children exist, not living upon this earth no, but still. Why do they venture to my castle? What is their desire here?" I rose to my feet and looked to the heavens. "I will no longer cower at your presence; I am worthy to speak! Answer me this, what does it all matter, if anything? Am I Evil or am I saved? I can no longer mange this life under a lack of understanding. ANSWER ME!"

Nothing.

"Thou shall not tempt the Lord thy God; Tempting I am not! Father I simply ask for understanding, is this lawlessness?"

I stood in silence.

"As I thought."

I left the worship chamber and made my way into the kitchen.

I opened the cupboard and stared with longing into a bottle of red wine and could taste the liquid dripping already in my saliva. I allowed the reruns to play… Debauchery, hangovers, regrets, and all folly. I had suppressed the memories of my youth so strongly over the years I more so recall blurry waves of static than anything else. I had a fit of rage brewing inside that I feared I could not contain but somehow, some way, I mustered enough strength to walk away from the cabinet and continue my sobriety.

"Few more days, and I shall be free of this place, I will not drown in anger but climb clear minded to my freedom."

I sank into a saddened state and depressed the intensities into emptiness and made my way to an uninterruptible sleep.

CHAPTER 16.

Before the rise of the warming sun, I set off out of the castle, slipping through the trees and quickly disappearing from the sight of God. I decided it best to leave unannounced so as not to alarm the demons that collect about my manor. Bags in hand I walked with a demanding haste due north to the docks eighty-three miles dead ahead.

"Where are you going?" an unfamiliar voice chirped.

"Who's there?" I scanned the woods,

"So, you're Damien, you look like you just crawled out of a goat barn." She giggled.

"Show yourself demon." I ordered.

"Demon? Is that what you think of us then?"

"Who are you?" I shook.

A beautiful young lady aged roughly twenty stepped a mere five feet in front of me, she did not come from the trees or in a particular direction… she came from the air all around.

"Lilith?" I trembled.

"Very good, my mom said you were sort of dumb, but I think she underestimates you."

"You are not allowed in this realm; your mother told me this."

"I didn't say she was smart either. I'm not allowed on the castle grounds, there is no restriction to the forest."

"What is your desire with me?"

"Desire? No, no…" she began to circle me, like a wolf intimidating it's pray. "I guess I have them daddy issues, I hear the other girls whining about."

I did not respond but allowed her rambling to continue.

"I suppose you have no questions for me? tossing me in a fire merely seconds after I was born, I don't suppose you've thought about me?"

Again, I did not respond.

"Well, I can see where Mark gets his attitude. Pity he admires you so much, if only he knew how you treated his sisters… hell, how you treat all women."

I held my empty demeanor and waited for the beast to leave me.

"You know Damien, when we go to heaven, we are given a permanent age. We do not have a say, it's more of a randomly generated number and that's what we get. I was just lucky enough to land on twenty. The twins eleven, what a shame… they might easily be swayed by you but not I. I take unkindly to this silent treatment; but like my mother, I can do all the talking, if need be, however…"

I remained inactive.

"Fair enough, since you wish to not engage with me, maybe I'll go ask Samantha to do it for me."

"No, no, no, no I am here for discussion certainly." I coward.

"Mmm, I see Samantha holds dominion over you. Good to know." She grinned.

"What is it you want?" I impatiently huffed.

"What is it I want? Hmm…" she toyed. "Well, I suppose I should ask why you threw me into the fire but, it kind of worked out I mean, who'd wanna live on this wretched earth raised by you? Hmm, What is it I want? Oh, I know."

I could see the sinister black fill her eyes and before vanishing from sight she hissed demonically.

"I just want to see you die."

From the air she came and into the air she leapt.

I ran through the woods at top speed, bags fell, and leaves crunched beneath my feet. I just ran and ran; I knew I could not escape my demons, but I felt the further I left the castle the more likely the odds I would not be found.

I was deep into the woods just as the sun began to set, I found a small cave like form inside a rock, I set aside what I still managed to carry. I pulled a fire-starting kit out and began collecting wood for the night.

The flames crackled and popped as the sun sank, and darkness engulfed the land. A strange dense fog flooded the surrounding trees and shadows and whispers lingered about.

"Lilith, I'm sure you are nearby, I can assure you I have known great horrors in my life, the forest does not scare me." I tempted. "Come join me at camp if you wish, no need for childish games."

My confidence turned to fright.

"Samantha." I beheld in terror.

She formed out of the darkness and sat across from me on the other side of the fire. She sat in silence and peered into my weak soul.

"Samantha I, I, I, you see," I stuttered incoherently. "We, just, we, we, well see."

She did not flinch in the slightest or give any indication of the slightest emotion.

I noticed she had aged to her mid-forties and yet still managed to keep her gorgeous features, as if she hadn't aged at all. I could only guess forties by the deeper wisdom she held in her eyes.

"I must confess my works." I gathered myself. "The deeds in which I performed upon you I can say with certainty was the will of the Lord, surly you know this?"

I felt myself levitate from my sitting log and violently I was thrust into a tree and crashed to the ground with great force. I fumbled about trying to gather back to my feet and I beheld a chorus of purples and reds, shapes, and demons crowding the air around me.

They tore at my robes and kicked and beat me mercilessly, I held my hands up to protect my face, but I could feel them bash the heels of their boots into my skull until blood pooled beneath me. when at once the mob disappeared into the night.

I squirmed in pain and tried to collect my wits, but the dizzy stars rattled about, and the throbbing pain persisted deeply.

Just when I thought the madness was over, Samantha bludgeoned me with a large stick, and while dazed, she tied my hands behind my back, then bent me over a log.

"Now you will feel my pain." She spoke.

She pulled a glowing stob from the fire and jabbed the red-hot end into my anal cavity and proceeded to penetrate me repeatedly with the glowing end. I had never screamed in such agony in my entire life.

There I was left, ass up, bleeding, beaten, and defiled.

"Hahahaha, Looks like you and Samantha had some fun." Lilith mocked.

"hu, ha, ssss" I whispered incoherently, broken and in excruciating pain.

"Exactly what I thought you'd say" She laughed. "Well, I'm glad Samantha had her fun with you before you die, makes me happy that's for sure." She squatted in front of me and looked into my eyes. "I could kill you now, but, suffering, oh suffering, well… it's so much more enjoyable to watch."

She slapped me in the face and as the pressure connected, she vanished once more.

I folded off the log and drug myself to the fire side. I curled up in a ball like a beaten dog and visions of Kulsin began to play in pristine clarity. My hands trembled as the intolerable abuse left its impression, the nerves damaged, and the roaring burn inflamed deep in my bowls endured.

"Father, dare I speak? If I am tested like thy servant Job, I beg for endurance oh Lord."

I shivered although the fire raged, I watched the shadowing flames dance upon the rock wall and prayed for sleep.

CHAPTER 17.

I was unable to walk without aid and I tried to pull myself up with the help of a stick or the face of a rock but was unable to stand after such violent abuse. I crawled away from the horrific scene and continued north hoping to regain my strength to stand before long. My vison was weak as my eyes had nearly swollen shut from the attack.

I could hear the gentle roar of a creek nearby and pulled myself down the bank and got a much-needed drink.

"Father" I called but continued to speak no more.

I tore at the weeds that protruded from the bank and was able to make it back up the small hill side. I crawled and crawled, until I reached a wall of thick brush. I felt the piercing stab of every stick and stob as I crawled through the tangled mess.

"AHHHHHHHH!" I screamed in broken disbelief.

There, dead ahead, was the castle.

"Am I to be merely tortured then, is this for your amusement Lord?"

I felt a hand begin to pull at my shoulder and help raise me to my feet.

"Is it you Lord?" I exhaled.

The small stature and fact I was met with silence made me realize it had to be Mark.

"Bless you son." I proclaimed with excitement. "I promise I will make it up to you, as soon as I am able to walk alone."

Mark helped me back to the castle and once inside I crawled again into a bottle of red wine.

"You see what a man gets for following the Lord boy" I slurred. "I have been dealing with silence all my life… I *hiccup* I've been dealing with a demon and his name is *hiccup* GOD. Now oh no that is not all" I took a big swing. "WHORES boy, WHORES all women are WHORES; lying, manipulating, deceitful creatures… *hiccup* promise *hiccup* Promise me boy you will keep away from them – unless of course they are caged up *hiccup* and used at will. I can tell you, when I *hiccup* first arrived at this castle *hiccup* I was much more than I am today, *hiccup* I was a man of… Well… a man, no doubt!"

I was looked upon with silence as usual.

"Well damn it boy, say something! *hiccup* what's with this mute behavior… mutiny, mutate, muter *hiccup* Now again I swore id leave this dreadful place *hiccup* but here I am once more *hiccup* GOD CURSED ME – SATAN CURSED ME!"

My nodding head could take no more and I finally passed out from the alcohol.

I raised my head from the stone floor and wiped away the vomit that drooled from the edge of my mouth as I pressed my hand against my throbbing head. My intestines burned in pain and my inability to walk still a reality.

"MARK" I screamed. "Another bottle."

I scanned the area and realize I was alone.

"DAMN BOY, MUST I DO EVERYTHING!"

I crawled my way into the kitchen and the foul stench of rotting meat filled the air. Flies swarmed over a slab of subhuman pork, I ignored the matter and pulled myself to the liquor cabinet.

I downed as many bottle as I could possibly ingest before passing out cold once more.

"Estavon" a faint voice whispered in my ear.

"Mother?" I slurred.

"My son, why do you disappoint me so?"

"I've tried, I've tried mother and I" I began to choke on my regurgitation and could barely fight for air.

"I should have fed you to the fire at birth."

I was unable to speak as the gagging intensified. I could only give a rebuttal in my mind and it to began to fade.

Just before death came to my door I slunked forward and the vomit ejected from my mouth and all over my robes.

I could not feel - as I had numbed my senses, however I could predict the inevitable end; my God a shell of a man and

I felt the defeat flow as I began urinating in my robes.

"Is… This… Your… Will…. Father?"

I puked once more and drenched my entire body in the acidic spew of wine and stomach fluid. I laughed and I mocked, I cried, and I scolded. I felt the years collapse inside me like an avalanche of frozen emotion, cold, burning and painfully obvious.

I tilted my eyes ahead and noticed Mark and Mary Ann sitting across from me staring at my wreckage.

"Demons, Demons, get thee behind me Satan…. Lucifer… Beelzebub." I faded in and out of consciousness.

In the darkest depths of my soul – the soul of a wretched man, whose life held no more than misery, sorrow and regret I had finally arrived at a solution, an answer, and absolute must.

"I can tell you kids *hiccup* it's important; you see me? You see this, now this isn't talk this is *hiccup* Prophecy from the almighty... now listen, important you got it *hiccup*"

I finally passed out cold as my body compressed into the massive pile of vomit, I bathed it.

My eyes flashed open for a second, I was unaware of the time as a whole or the past several hours for that matter. Time slipped by, I could not grasp reality or dream, fact, or fiction.

I blinked and at one glimpse I saw the two kids and at another I saw a trash can and a plant. I could hear the voice of women and priests screaming inside my mental chamber and I was confounded by my insecurities. I wasn't sure what made sense and what didn't, simple confusion from alcohol or hallucination by schizophrenia. One thing was for certain I was floating with inebriations ghost but... I was perfectly clear minded of the state. Did I make sense? Well... I don't know.

"What trickery is this?" I slurred.

I tried to crawl out of the room but wasn't even able to raise a single limb. Then once more my eyes shut for some time.

BBBLLLAAAAHHHH, I let out a massive exorcism of vomit and shit my robes all at the same time.

"Your will Lord" I insulted.

The garbage can and plant were no longer visible, and I saw Mark just across from me wide eyed and deranged. He pulled a knife out of the floor and began to slowly slit his throat. Blood poured from the slash and his eyes held the same wide character and I blinked to behold a garbage can.

"Toying Father?"

The smell of vomit and shit forced me to throw up a little more and I pissed in my robes again adding to the already rotting meat smell that was still present in the chamber.

Awakening for this blip in time, I was able to crawl ever so slightly to a less contaminated area. Shit streaked across the floor and the watery mix of urine and vomit trailed along with me.

"Is this your worst?" I laughed.

My eyes rolled in my skull, and I reached for a bottle but passed out cold, this time not waking for some time.

CHAPTER 18.

Trapped in limbo, hurled down into the bottomless pit – I was barely conscious when I heard the familiar banging.

Knock knock

"Away with you demon." I managed.

I felt a burning itch deep in my rectum - assuming my shit must have started an infection. With pain and determination, I pulled myself up to my feet and took baby steps to the door.

Knock knock

"I am coming Satan!" I shouted, spit flying from my mouth. I held the wall and whatever else would carry me to the door.

Knock knock

"Damn you!" my patience wearing thin.

I pulled open the door and there before me stood Victoria, flesh hanging from bone, decomposing and mute.

I did not speak with her but simply ran my eyes over her in investigation.

"Satan's games, I have no love to mourn, I will not be manipulated with such evil." I slammed the door.

I stared at the solid wood for some time before curiosity won me over.

The door creaked open slowly and as I expected, nothing but the wind.

I slammed the door shut and creeped my way down the hall and into the medical chamber. The flaming infection hidden deep in my innards was harboring all of my thoughts.

I finally managed my way and pulled a tube of ointment I had concocted some time ago and emptied the content into my anal cavity.

"Father." I mumbled as I felt a gentle cool of relief.

I stretched my back to a straighter posture and walked about allowing the cream to do its work.

"Damien." Voices plagued the air.

"Get thee behind me Satan." I roared as I continued my laps.

"Damien."

"When on the vast sea, I sail to the shore, an angel of heaven welcomes me home..." I sang as loud as I could to tune out the voices.

"Estavon."

"La, la la, luh la la, la, la la, luh la la."

I felt a multitude of hands clutch tightly to my robes and I was dragged out of the chamber and down the hall at a violent speed.

"RELEASE ME DEMONS." I pleaded.

My body was skipped off every step that lead down into the dungeon, smashing into the door below.

A fierce wind blew the doors open and I was tossed inside, and the door locked behind me.

"Reduce me to cattle then Lord?" I shouted.

The subhumans screamed and pleaded for food and fresh water. I took the wooden bucket from the hook and began making my rounds – it was not from sympathy that I doubled their ration but out of fear of losing my cattle to illness.

As I reached cell four, inside I was haunted to the very core of my being.

"Damein…Estavon…Damein…" voices rang in unison.

All of them present, Victoria, Samanth, Mark, Mary Ann, Lilith, my mother, and every soul from Kulsin, crammed packed in the small cell.

I was in such terror I could only stare frozen at the hellish display.

But one face in particular stood from the rest.

"Angela." I softly spoke.

I unlocked the cell door and without fear nor hesitation walked through the demonic ghosts of my past and straight to her side.

I extended my hand, and she reached out and floated gently upon my skin. I looked into her beautiful face and remember every feature so clearly; it was as if she had been in front of me and never left all those years ago. We were not bullied nor harassed in any way by cell mates.

I leaned down to kiss her and, in the process, she vanished into the air.

I had not experienced such peace in all of my life, every good memory of Victoria faded and was overtaken by the memories of Angela.

I fell to my knees inside my lonely cell and after smashing my face into my hands I looked up and there before me stood Victoria.

"Who was she to you, that you love her over me?" she humbly asked.

"I had found her in my mind inside the walls of Kulsin." I answered. "She was once a transparent figure like yourself, yet she became to me so real, I loved her without remorse."

"I see her memory has begun to erase mine."

"It is not of my will to do so, but I am overruled by God."

"And what then of your children Estavon?"

"MY NAME IS DAMIEN!" I screamed.

"And what of your children Damien?"

"I HAVE NO CHILDREN! I have no flesh that walks this earth from my body to physical being. I am a lonely monk and no more."

"What am I to you?" she began to sob.

"You are a demon, sent to tempt me - from the fires of hell you have brought a plague upon my castle."

"Is it then your will to die alone?"

"It is not my will, but the will of the Father."

Without another word, she was gone.

I searched the cell for Angela, but I was unsuccessful.

"Wander me in the desert Father, starve me in the wilderness... I will enter the promise land and I will have my milk and honey along with wine and adultery. I am not evil that I pursue the subhuman female

I have been delt. What more can a humble man do if his eyes cannot fall upon a woman with lust… I may create love, but you will not take her image from me!”

I ran from the cell and started to bang on the exit doors and resorted to grabbing a club to try and smash my way out of the dungeon to no avail.

“AAAHHHHHHHH” I screamed in desperation.

“Is it enough to rid me of my imagination father that you must reduce me to cattle?”

I was met with silence.

“I wish not to degrade myself Lord, I have tried for decades to please you only to be brought to the subhuman level and mocked. I have taken on more burden then I can now bear Father. I BEG YOU FOR FREEDOM OH LORD!”

One of the cattle dare to speak to me.

“Damien, that is your name, yes? Come to my cell, the Lord has given me his word to share with you.”

I looked into the man’s eyes and could see his sincerity. With caution I slugged towards him.

“Closer, just closer now…”

I was a mere foot away and watched as he hurled a yellow ball of mucus from his lips and smacked me dead center in the face.

“God says fuck off you sick bastard.”

Everyone in the dungeon began to roar in laughter and the humiliation sent me into a fit.

CHAPTER 19.

Madness entered my mind once more and I could no longer contain the grim reality God had delt me and I longed for an end to my suffering.

I did not retaliate against the cattle by offering the same insult, but instead I smiled and the fear in the subhumans eyes brought on more joy then what would have been obvious pay back.

"The fires of hell await you." I spoke in a demonic cadence. "All of you for that matter – all of us. The Lord has assured me this." I announced. "We shall begin the transition from this world to the next in due time; We shall fast for three days, and I suggest you all repent of your many sins on this earth." Silence fell throughout the dungeon and was replaced with tremendous fear. "So sayeth the Lord."

I walked down the cell block and around the wall where I would frequently hide my presence while I raped the subhuman beauties in private. I pressed a sequence of stones and the floor opened up revealing steps that led down to a dirty floor cellar and I proceeded down, the door sliding shut behind me.

Light from the furnace exposed a small room and I wandered over to a table and sat. My thoughts overwhelming and a mixture of clarity and anxiety trampled over me.

"My life Father has been met only with great suffering; I have known sorrows friendship for too long. I cannot feel the depths of my soul to pour out any worth wild sentiment, I am not certain that remorse is something I am truly capable of. I feel not your presence oh Lord, I pray now as a man attempting to relieve himself from a burden – if only to the wind. Perhaps unbeknownst to me, I have inadvertently been praying to Satan all along. Careless as the Lord has written - Whom of you by worrying could add a single hour to your life – Not that I miss understood, no, but for in worrying I might have been aware of my atrocity. Although I may understand now, once more I will say I feel no guilt or shame, therefore I find the need for repentance impossible, as honesty would not be present. Therefore, I believe I am in cahoots not with the Lord Jesus Christ, but with the prince of evil, that old serpent, Lucifer. If it be Gods hand in creation – in that he knows all – the fate of my life sealed; then I find it absolutely necessary to carry out my God given duty by turning to my rightful masters command without further contemplation."

Upon finishing my vow, I asked my new master for visitation from my father, of whom I've never met... and he obliged.

He appeared in a gentle smoke that rolled from the shadows and joined me at the small table sat directly across from me.

his hair black, eyes pale, and a long dark beard fell into his black robes.

"Father?"

"Who are you? What is this place?" he searched with his eyes.

"I am your son Damien."

"You fool, I have no son." His voice was rough and grizzly.

"My mother's name was Gisel."

He stopped searching momentarily and looked at me with a grin.

"Ah, yes, the hill street prostitute, who could forget her. You know boy your mother was a wild whore; she'd let you stick it in her ass then suck you off immediately after." He laughed. "Never knew she had a child... are you sure I'm the father? She had a lot of dick that one."

"I am sure, listen, I just wanted to ask you something." I hesitated.

"Go on then…"

"Although I was very young, I recall my mother saying she was going to find you and you would help get her on her feet so that she could come back for me while I stayed in Kulsin, did she do this?"

"I'm telling you your mother was a whore boy! Did she not tell you I died in a war as well… she was mad!"

"That is not the answer to my question." I looked at him with growing anger.

"Mmmmm… The truth may hurt you boy, are you sure you seek it?"

"The truth is better than a lie, no matter how painful."

"Very well… She did find me, I was in the back of an old beer chamber called Havensgrow, she came in and interrupted a meeting I was having with two young girls and started to accuse me of being a father to one of her demon babies. I did not take her interruption lightly, but instead of an outburst, I suggested she go with me to my private room to talk. Once I had her inside, I strangled her until her eyes popped out of her socks and then I fucked her in the ass after she had left this world.”

With all the force I could drive from my body, I took a swing at the old bastard and my hand was met with the thin air.

Alone once more in a new sea of anguish and betrayal, I cried the tears of a broken soul until exhaustion won the better of me.

 “Don’t cry my son.”

“Mother?” I lifted my head from the table and there she sat across from me.

“Your father is an evil man no doubt but, you should not let his words hurt you so.”

"How can you say this after what he has done to you? He deserves to rotten in hell!" I cried.

"I assure you he most definitely is" she smiled.

"Mother, what am I to do, help me."

"you know the answer son, it is inside you, look inside your poor black heart."

She vanished as if she had never been there to begin with.

"Is there no more visitors' master? If there be send them now so that I may rest."

The smoke was not black this time but an oozing green, as it settled there across from me, I was surprised to see myself in exact form.

We did not speak right away, but for some time we stared. I did not know what to say, given the great deal of silence I could still not think of a worthy question to ask myself. My other form glared waiting for a response, but I had nothing to offer. Finally, he broke the silence.

"Do you feel inside you an enemy or a saint? Does it fascinate you or is that same voice the reason for your burden? Now… I can assure you that one is more powerful than the other – of course you know this but – it is that time where you must succumb to one or the other, this grey area is no more, the book has closed."

"If the book has sealed my fate well then… in fear I ask… in what book has my name been written?"

He did not answer verbally but responded with a demonic grin then vanished before my eyes.

I sat alone in the agonizing truth and spent the rest of the night in isolated emptiness. I longed to contemplate a proper way out of my misery but was time and time again broken by the grim reality that I must obey my masters orders.

"MASTER, SHOW YOURSELF!"

I was met with silence.

"Do you also cower from my presence?" I insulted, hoping to get a rise.

I was met with silence.

"As pathetic as my last God you are, well I can handle life then on my own from here on out!" I commanded.

My energy level spiked to an all-time low, and though I wished to call upon my adversary I passed out before I was given a chance.

CHAPTER 20.

I fell into a deep sleep and neither did I dream nor wince, my head, and arms flat on the desk and thick drool pooled at the edge of my lips. The dancing shadows sent from the furnace to the stone wall flickered in silence just above the cold dirt floor. The smell of earth and heat inhaled into my nostrils and exhaled back into the cellar at a gentle pace. I could hear the angelic voice of a seraph singing to me a lullaby of peace and freedom – I had not heard such beautiful acapella in all my life. The voice grew in its volume and by its brilliance sounded as though an entire choir harmonized in perfect unison, performing the most immaculate symphony one could dare dream. I felt the dark void of light sway in the captivating melody, and I praised the creature for its talented gift. I moved to the majestic sound of holy power and wished to bask in the glory forever. When at once, the call of my Master did sound.

"Damien." The frozen hiss of death whispered in my ear.

"Master." I respond trembling.

"I have known you my son since birth, I can guide you to an eternity of freedom."

"You must tell me who sings to me Master?"

"Tis I, my son."

"Glorious you are Master; praise be to you." I spoke in awe.

"I call to you, my son; I call you home."

"Yes Master, I wish to join you."

"Come Home." His voice echoed as it faded into the darkness.

"I will, Master."

I arose from sleep and walked my way back to address the cattle.

"Subhuman cattle, My master has spoken to me to proclaim your freedom from your shackles, freedom from your cage, you will walk in the name of Lucifer in the promised land for all eternity."

The cattle gasped in their cells and the look of horror fell upon all their faces.

"Do not be afraid, For the Master of old does not come to bring fear, but freedom. I shall now sacrifice my body for your pleasure, as promise to you of your delivery from your prison."

I disrobed and started at cell one; the children took turns at my flesh, clawing, tearing, raping, and mutilating my flesh. I felt the pain of crucifixion as I proudly had twenty-four more cells to deliver. The cattle barked and spit, urinated and hurled feces at my open wounds. I was beaten until the stars hung bright in the night of my minds exposed sky, mercilessly and without a single who did not join in on the torture.

"Have me you animals, if it be the will of my Master." I shouted.

I was handed off to the final cell and I was in unrecognizable shape. Through the squint of my swollen eyes, I could just make out Mark standing there watching me passed around, - finally with a satisfied smile upon his face.

"I love you, Father." He spoke.

His words provided me with enough strength to understand my act had not been in vain. I tugged away from the final cell and slugged my way down the block with insults and hurling.

"Master, It is done." I mumbled in extraordinary pain.

I laid naked and blood soaked near the exit doors and asked Master if I could be

freed from the dungeon for a short time...
he obliged.

The doors opened and I crawled up the stairs to my great hall and made my way to the worship room.

I creaked open the door and without hesitation, I pulled a torch from the chamber wall and set the room ablaze.

"Master, I welcome you to castle grotesque, your earthly home."

The fires reduced all of the "Lords" shrines into ash and the dark pupils of my eyes magnified in the flames.

"IS THIS YOUR WILL OH LORD" I laughed in insanity.

The crackling of the flames were overpowered by a tremendous storm of thunder and lighting brewing outside the castle. Rain poured and seeped through the cracked stoned ceiling and the high voltage electricity strobed through the windows in an extreme flash.

"DO YOUR WORST!" I taunted.

The earth quaked beneath me, and the castle shook violently.

"Hahahahahahahahaha!"

I slammed the door shut to the worship room, walked into the kitchen, and pulled the last remaining bottle of red wine I had in the castle.

"To the death of the Father and to the Freedom of will." I chugged the content, afterward smashing the bottle to the stone floor – glass exploded just as the lighting struck and I could just begin to hear the Seraph start to sing.

"Rise loud, sing to me Master."

I marched back down the hallway and kicked open the door to the dungeon.

"IT IS TIME!" I announced to the cattle. Their fear was great beyond compare.

I walked down into the cellar and started gathering kegs of powder I had stored for such occasions. Each barrel held ten gallons of powder and I had fifty-five in storage.

I took one of the barrels and began to pour the black grains onto the stone path; making sure that each cell was properly piled. One by one I grabbed another barrel until the entire chamber was completely swimming in in powder.

The cattle screamed in fear and the thunder intensified.

"I shall now offer you as sacrifice to the dark God Lucifer. You shall taste freedom once more."

I grabbed a torch and placed it on a wooden bucket and new I had about two minutes to leave the chamber before the bucket burnt into the powder trail and the dungeon would be no more.

I had emptied fifteen barrels and stacked the remaining barrels around the chambers main support and new the above floor would crash down and send every living soul inside directly to hell.

"Bon voyage, human swine." I gave a bow and made my way out of the dungeon, shutting off the lights and locking the door behind me for good measure.

I could hear the cattle screaming through the thick walls as I made my way up the stairs; I reached the great hall as a tremendous earth-shattering boom echoed though out the castle.

I could hear as planned the stone floor crumble and crash to the ground below stifling every subhuman scream until the chamber was exposed to silence.

"THY WILL BE DONE!" I shouted.

But before I had time to celebrate my triumph. A voice broke though the thundering storm outside and I was forced to my knees and face planted into the cold stone. The voice was inaudible, yet I felt great understanding of my abominations and perversion. I was hardened in my heart and felt no remorse for my deeds. The voice left me, and I felt a great fear sweep over my being.

I raised my head and could see cracks begin to carve their way up the stone wall and the shaking of the earth grew more frightful.

I rose to my feet and ran with all my pathetic strength and the ceiling and walls began to crumble down around me.

"MASTER SAVE ME!" I begged.

I could see the exit door just insight and as I reached for the door handle, a stone came crashing down, pinning me to the floor.

"MASTER, I IMPLORE THEE, SAVE ME!"

I twisted my head and beheld a great heavy stone break free from the roof above and gravity had it in course for my skull.

"Father, Lord in heaven save me." I uttered in desperation.

In the brief moment before death, I realized my folly. I could hear the knocking of demons and see the atrocities I had performed in my lifetime, I could dare say I felt the semblance of remorse, if only for a second. Reflected upon me the eyes of demons and I could not ask them for mercy, for I knew all to well the dealing of punishment.

BOOM!

CHAPTER 21.

I crawled from the rubble, coughing, and hacking up dust and debris. I made it outside and I laid on the steps trying to regain my consciousness. I was not in pain nor was I bleeding, in fact I felt nothing at all.

"Thank you Master." I praised.

I raised my head to look about the area and was overwhelmed with terror.

Darkness plagued the scene, fires, ash, and vast desolation, I was thrust into the nightmare and a creature in all black robes stood before me.

"Damien." It hissed. "Walk with me." It turned and I was forced to follow.

"What is this place?" I trembled.

"Why, this what you've always dreamed of, is it not?"

"I'm frightened, please return me to my castle." I pleaded.

"Look there." It pointed to a pile of rock and dust. "That is all that remains of your castle."

I gasped in horror and the creature took me by the shoulder and hauled me to the rubble.

"There." It pointed.

Just beneath a heavy pile of stone, I noticed some blood and chunks clinging to the rock.

"What is this?"

"Remember." It hissed.

A vision did fall over me, and I could recall a large rock slab crashing into my skull, and I fell to my knees in despair.

"Does this mean…" I choked on my words.

"Ah, yes, it means that you are mine now… for all eternity." The creature grinned.

"FATHER, I CALL TO THEE OH LORD!" I screamed in desperation.

The creature just laughed and began to pull me over the ruins; as we fell through the rock and into where the dungeon did lay, he assured me.

"God is not here."

There was the smallest gap, just large enough to pace around maybe ten steps. The creature sat me on the floor and stood before me.

"What do you want with me?" I cried.

"I want what you wanted in life, eternal suffering. you shall remain in this castle for all times, bound by the grotesque actions you performed here, you will suffer in death as you caused suffering in life."

"NO, I BEG…." He vanished and I remained locked in the dungeon, In a shell of stone and subhuman death.

"GOD PLEASE, SAVE ME!" I cried out repeatedly.

I was met with silence.

I rose to my feet and with adrenaline type haste, I began to peel away at the rock, trying to dig myself out the chamber to no avail.

There was no light, no air, I was forced to sit with my thoughts and dwell on the life I had lead before my untimely death. I could not panic, I could not feel sorrow, I was numb to all degrees of emotion aside from tremendous suffering.

I rocked back and forth, reliving all the moments of my life in excruciating detail. I could not call upon God for comfort, I was unable to break free from the bond of demonic possession.

I sat alone in my tomb and viewed my life on repeat, until I began to speak aloud to myself to break the endless silence.

"Creature! Are you near? I have replayed my life, although dark and viewed by others as repulsive, I find no fault with my actions, for my actions were learned from the world. I had no guidance in morality, nor did I understand its mystery. Father in heaven did I not seek you and simply not understand – am I to be faulted for lack of knowledge? Sent to hell for all eternity? I am however guilty of ignorance, for had I known my fate I would have died long ago. Now I sit, suffering a multitude of life's visions and I know now I would have ended life to dwell merely a few years of existence – had I known. What debt can a man like me repay when even in death he does not understand his suffering? Am I simply a toy in a cruel game? From what do I know of other peoples understanding when my adult life was spent in isolation, the cattle did not communicate with me nor I with them? Was it I who sent them to the castle? Why do you hold their vision so strongly upon me? may the dark creature who brought me here return for a proper judgement and not be so quick to condemn?"

I paced around my tomb counting to ten upon landing on my starting point. I watched the rock begin to stain white as a path cut into the stone. I walked and walked, polishing the rock below me and could not feel the sands of time, a day was like year and a year like a day. My emptiness did not shift at all for I could not feel moods, I simply spun in circles and sat on the cold stone.

I could hear whispers and screaming, all incoherent and not amusing in the slightest degree. I sat back down on the floor and rocked back and forth and did my time.

"Mark?" I called. "Mary Ann, Victoria?" I knew they were free to roam about in the after life and figured maybe they would find me and teach me how to transport between realms.

I continued to call for them but never received an answer.

"Ungrateful lot!... CREATURE, SHOW YOURSELF!" I attempted once more to only be met with silence.

I understood that no one would come and that my fate was to be locked in this prison, so I laid down and shut my eyes – basking in silences and the endless embrace of numb emotion, I simply succumbed to my punishment.

**

"Alright we're gonna start right here, here, bring that over here and remove these rocks!" a voice muffled into my chamber.

"Who's there?" I called.

I could hear the grinding and crumbling of rock being excavated above me and waited for the voices to free me.

The beeping siren carved its way into the rubble and a small light shone through to my prison. A large claw like beast stretched its arm and tore away at the rock and I was able to climb my way out of the dust.

"Thank you, thank you." I grabbed at the men who freed me but became quickly aware I did not exist to them.

My hands fell through them, and my words fell on def ears. I looked about the area and the sun did shine, and the forest grown, all though unfamiliar to my eyes. new growth that must have taken decades to spring forth and I wondered about searching for a clue.

A sign where the entrance to my castle once lay read.

This is the site of the infamous

Damien Uriah Estavon.

Castle Grotesque

Coming soon.

Bizarre machinery unlike anything I had ever seen crawled about the land and roads and colorful signs adorned my property.

"What is this?" I mumbled.

I examined the sign I had just read closer and upon further inspection I noticed a small group of numbers.

4-9-2024

"Father." I shuttered.

I had gone to my prison in the spring of six hundred and sixty-seven and I woke in a strange new time.

I ran.

I ran with all of my ability; I could feel no fatigue and my numb character allowed me to run at my heart's desire. I turned back to gauge my distance traveled and I was shocked to find I had not made any progress of any kind.

Bound then by a creature of unprecedented power, I was shackled to my home, and I could never leave its place.

I gave up quickly and retired on a pile of stacked rock and I watched the might of the human machinery, claw and remove every inch of my manor.

I watched them gather as my skeletal remains were uncovered as I eavesdropped on their discussion.

"It's gotta be him, its gotta be!" they exclaimed excitedly. "Jim come look at this, this has to be Damien wouldn't you say."

Thirty-two men and women gathered to gawk at my bones. I heard them cheer in delight and carefully gather every fragment of me and haul me away in a white machine.

"What Satanism is this oh Lord; you bring a cult of demon worshippers to my home to belittle me?"

I watched them work day and night and soon the remains of my castle were long gone, and a new group arrived to begin erecting an exact replica of my castle.

I looked over the shoulder of one gentleman called John as he held a large blue piece of parchment with an inaccurate layout of my castle.

"Fools" I huffed.

They brought in dull stones and followed orders and I watched as they rebuilt a foreign structure they claimed to be as superior and representative as my own.

I walked through the front door and was brought into an open chamber with glass cases holding some of my worldly possessions. Silverware, clothing, buckets and trunk pieces, a club I used for cattle control and various other items. Little signs indicating these were in fact my possessions.

I stepped into each room, some unfinished while others looked nothing like my home in their completion. No high tower, no medical chamber, and my kitchen was in the back of the castle while the library was in the front. My great hallway was not present at all and where the worship room once was now sat a chamber filled with marketable items one could take home upon purchase.

In just twenty-four hours, there was talk of this place being infested by excited admirers of myself and If I was capable of emotion, I would be in disgust.

"Are we ready for tomorrow." A voice announced. "We are estimated to have as many as three hundred people here tomorrow, possibly more, remember to direct them to the gift shop if possible and guides, make sure you're on your gig, people really know their history of this place so be ready for hecklers. Alright team lets go home and have a good rest for tomorrows grand opening."

The place erupted in cheers, and I sat at one of the windows inside the castle as they all began to disperse – into what they call cars.

I sat in a chair looking off into what faintly resembled Ehpoe Forest and I longed for a release from this eternal prison.

"Though the winds change, and the night shows no stars, I cannot feel nor cry out, for the Lord above has gone and the demons below have left me. I was formed from the dust, and I had a time of being.

The brevity of life has proven true, for in the blink of an eye, I now wait in eternity more alone than ever before. Oh Lord, I am and always have been… Nothing.”

CHAPTER 22.

I could see for miles as I sat atop the newly designed castle. Cars backed up and loud horns blasted, and voices rang out in what was moments ago peaceful air.

"Sick creatures, do they not see their folly." I stated.

Hordes of them gathered outside of the castle walls and a man holding a giant pair of scissors sniped a long red cloth and the people cheered.

I walked back into the main chamber while the crowds were still held back from entering. To the left of the room was a set of long stairs that led into the dungeon, and I walked down. I counted an even number of steps and once again ignored the inaccuracy. I pushed open the door and was surprised they achieved the creaking noise my old door made. Once inside I looked

about and counted twenty cells and –
although five less than what I had I was
happy to see the dungeon replicated my
own with a high level of accuracy. I could
almost hear the subhumans coughing and
whining for release. I walked up and down
the hall and reminisced in empty feeling of
the days of old. Long gone though they
were, it felt as if it were yesterday, I was
patrolling the cell block.

I stuck out my hand and it made no
noise as a skipped it across the bars of the
cell, I turned and made my way over to the
exit door and waited for the crowds to flood
in.

"Dude, I'm so stoked bro, this guy was
a fuckin nut job man."

"Yeah, no doubt, wild shit bro, this place is
gonna be badass."

I couldn't understand these people, they spoke in unintelligent form and their behavior was disrespectful in all manner.

I watched them hit each other and call names, push, shove, and curse as they all piled into the castle. They had strange flashing devices in their hands they seemed to obsess over, and they pointed them at the glass display and captured an image of the items and stored them somehow on their device.

It wasn't long before a fight broke out as one man claimed another bumped into his woman and the man ended up punching the other man repeatedly until four men in matching clothing tore them apart. One man was dragged from the building and the other was free to roam about as usual. While on the other side of the main chamber I saw a lady carving her name into the stone wall with a small metal object, her child touching the glass at every display they passed.

Voices cursed and shouted, and I watched on in disbelief. I noticed some had robes like my own and clothing with my image pasted on the front and some even had me inked into their skin. They paraded around laughing and joking with one another, completely amused by the actions I had carried out on this ground and in my life.

"Dude, bro you gotta come check this out."

"Wooooah"

"Bro, this is the club he used to like fuckin, bash peoples skulls in and shit."

"That's gnarly as fuck bro."

"I heard he like, fucked over a thousand girls and like caged them up in the basement and fuckin just had them whenever he wanted."

"That's badass bro."

"Right, dude he's like my hero man."

If only they knew the reality of my life, the torment and ultimate suffering I endured.

"Oh, my Lord." I heard one lady preach. "This is one twisted mother fucker man, uh uh, I ain't wanting to see no more of this shit, no thank you Jesus."

Well – I thought to myself. At least one person has some sense.

"Mom, can I get a shirt please?"

"Ok, but just one."

"But mom."

"No Damien, I don't want to argue, you can have one like we agreed on."

"Ok."

Mothers named their children after me and men and woman idolized and despised me. I could not believe what I was seeing but then a large white sheet fell from the ceiling and a man announced they would show a reenactment of all my atrocities.

I watched as the lights dimmed and a strange light flashed upon the cloth and a man who resembled me began to act out what was to be believed my life.

The crowd oohed and awed, gasped, and cheered, jumped and marveled. The man portraying me raped, butchered, and cannibalized for the audience and at the very end of the dramatization they clapped and cheered.

"What sick world is this, Father?"

I could hear the crowds joy in their approval of the event as they continued to look at displays and buy souvenirs, I made my way out of the rafters and began to walk among them. The people slipped through my transparent form, and I was merely a specter among them.

I came upon a booth serving alcohol and I tried with every fiber of my being to grab a cup but was not successful in my endeavor.

I continued my walk and the crowds roared and cussed, I noticed attractive women – none like I had ever before seen, walking around admiring my life and some even saying how they would have been a willing participant in my rape if I was still around today.

Others captured images of themselves strapped in pillory's, locked themselves in shackles, and painted their faces with blood while another held a club in their hands.

I found my way to the entrance door and stepped outside to look upon the faces of those waiting to get inside for their own entertainment.

"Father what kind of evil is this, am I to believe this real? Or is this a trick fashioned by the demons of hell?"

I looked into the sky and as I got lost in the cacophony of voices and the emptiness of my spirit, I could faintly make out a voice.

The voice was angelic and beautiful by all measure and the gentle lullaby it sang called me from the darkest recesses of my imagination and I was mesmerized by its grandeur.

The crowds continued to brush by, and I was glued to the sky. The voice ever so slowly increased its volume and sounded as if a choir had introduced itself to the fold. I sat in awe of it's holy nature and in that moment convinced myself that maybe, possibly, the Lord was coming to set me free from this prison.

The people, oblivious to the holy spirit, continued their happy go lucky time and as I began to lock deeper into my trance, I realized the nature of the voice and I recalled hearing it a long time ago and I was aware the call from this particular voice was disguised in beauty, but the reality was death.

The clouds began to swirl above, and a distant bolt of lightning flashed, and I knew what was to come.

Thunder began to roll, and the people paid no attention to the warning in the sky. They were so lost in their conformity; I was unsure if they could even be awakened.

Boom!

A bolt of lightning crashed into a nearby tree and the crowd reacted in gasps and they all began to pile into the castle. A fire broke out, people pointed and screamed as just then - a loud crack of thunder erupted in the skies and rain began to pour while darkness engulfed the scene. Children began to scream and cry in fear and clench their parents tightly.

"Its just a passing storm, everyone please remain calm, we can all gather inside until it passes, do not be alarmed." A voice echoed throughout the castle.

I could hear the seraph sing no more while instead I was plagued with a legion of demonic voices cascading into my thoughts forcing me to smash my fists into my ears and I begged God for silence.

The earth began to shake and the screams and pleas of those inside the castle escalated to an all-time high.

"God, Jesus save us."

"I promise if you get me out of this, I will change my ways."

"Yeah bro, this tight as fuck man."

"Hail Satan!"

The mixed emotion caused more chaos, as some began to attack others and lute and vandalize. Display cases were shattered, and noses were broken – still the storm raged, growing in intensity.

"FATHER FORGIVE THEM, THEY KNOW NOT WHAT THEY DO!" I pleaded their case but was met with no response to the matter.

I looked off into the distance and I could see figures, red and purple, dark, and demonic flickering from the wild fire, giving off the only light in this immense darkness.

A bolt of lightning pierced from the clouds and struck the grand opening sign and the crowd screamed in horror.

"REPENT BEFORE IT'S TOO LATE!" I screamed repeatedly upon def ears.

As terror gripped the minds of the people it was as if the Lord himself announced. "Peace be still!"

As quickly as the storm came it was gone.

The crowd chattered amongst each other and assured they were safe, some wishing to leave while others getting off on the thrill of danger.

I didn't understand why all this show was for nothing, it made no sense to me. Was it a warning? I couldn't say for sure.

"The storm has passed, there is no need to worry, please continue to enjoy your visit."

I watched as the sun cut through the clouds and the fires washed away by the aid of big red cars, the smoke rising into the air.

"Surly this can not be all Father?" I asked confused.

I hurried my way back into the castle. To my surprise the crowd seemed to have already forgotten the event and continued in their ways.

"Something is wrong with this damn door." I heard a man announce.

"Get me the crowbar, we may have to pry it open."

No one who arrived on the property remained outside but due to the storm they all gathered inside for shelter. I watched the men seem to have an impossible time at getting the door to open.

Meanwhile the crowd continued as usual, while a select few gave the door men a hard time cause they wanted to go outside and smoke.

A strange chill fell over me and I looked around trying to find the cause. I knew there had to be more to come but I couldn't understand what it could be.

"This door wont budge, it's starting to piss me off!"

Everyone was trapped inside the walls, and I began to connect the dots.

"Well, there is no back door in this place, we copied it exactly and he didn't have one, so we didn't make one."

"What about a cellar or something like that?"

"Well, he did have a dirt hole under the castle but, we new tourists wouldn't be allowed down there, so to save money we just didn't add it."

"So, you're sure this is the only exit?"

"Yep, this is it, I'm positive."

I walked over to a window by the front entrance and examined the land.

My eyes stretched above to the sky and to my immense horror, a thick cloud of demonic smoke circled about and gradually began to descend all around the castle, and I knew too well what that smoke was. For every individual inside these walls had demons, and I knew they loved revenge.

"REPENT, I SAY REPENT ALL OF YOU, THE TIME OF TROUBLE HAS COME UPON YOU!"

I watched the smoke take form into a legion of the most vile creatures one could ever imagine. They gathered like an army, surrounding the castle and all were ready to collect the soul that gave birth to them.

I looked around the castle and all the people had hardened their hearts, and although warned, none could be delivered. Their fate was sealed!

Knock Knock